GWENEVERE
AND THE
ROUND TABLE

WENDY BERG

SKYLIGHT
PRESS

Published in Great Britain in 2012 by Skylight Press, 210 Brooklyn Road,
Cheltenham, Glos GL51 8EA

Designed and typeset by Rebsie Fairholm
Publisher: Daniel Staniforth
Cover photo by Rebsie Fairholm

Printed and bound in Great Britain by Lightning Source, Milton Keynes
Typeset in Minion Pro. Titles are typeset in Origins and the Nelson family of
fonts designed by Laura Worthington

British Library Cataloguing in Publication Data.
A catalogue record for this book is available from the British Library.

www.skylightpress.co.uk

ISBN 978-1-908011-47-3

CONTENTS

CHAPTER ONE

Gwenevere, Faery Queen

THE LEGENDS of King Arthur, Queen Gwenevere, the knights of the Round Table and the quest for the Grail comprise one of the best-known mythologies of the western world. They hold a fascination that continues to inspire each new generation, and are constantly reinterpreted according to the ethos of the time. The names of King Arthur, Merlin, Lancelot, the Lady of the Lake and Morgan le Fey are familiar to most people, and even if we have not read the actual stories, we feel that we know them through the many recent films and television adaptations of the legends.

But alongside these well-known characters, Gwenevere is a comparatively shadowy figure who fails to make a distinctive impression on us. She seems to lack personality or purpose, and emerges as little more than a product of the conventions of her time. She is described as beautiful, kind and graceful, but so are most of the women who appear alongside her. The Arthurian legends are essentially stories of action: they describe men of courage who confront the challenges that arise in their defence of Arthur's kingdom and in their quest for the Mysteries of the Inner worlds where dragons, wild beasts and strange happenings are daily occurrences. Gwenevere naturally enough plays little part in the knights' heroic deeds in the lands of adventure, but she does not appear to provide a feminine complement to the otherwise predominately masculine energy of the stories. Even within the domestic environment of the court of the Round Table where she might perhaps have played a more definite role, we get little sense that she made any real contribution to the business of running the court or kingdom with her husband King Arthur. And because her character lacks definition, there is an inevitable tendency to interpret her as weak. Those who approach these legends in the hope of discovering the deeper message that lies therein are hard put to find much in the character of Gwenevere that offers them inspiration or guidance, or that reveals the role of the feminine Mysteries within the mythology.

Later interpretations of the legends have made much of Gwenevere's love affair with Lancelot, and over the centuries this has gradually become the most widely known aspect of her life, to the point where it is now almost impossible for the stories to be retold in fiction or film unless this relationship is made central to the plot. This is quite understandable: it provides her with a purpose and adds some passion to the stories which are otherwise a little lacking in romantic interest. But as an addition to the mythology the affair can scarcely be said to add any real depth of meaning.

When the legends are looked at in more detail, there are numerous gaps in our knowledge of Gwenevere that cannot easily be explained. Indeed, the more one tries to discover anything definite to say about her the more one encounters inexplicable lacunae. For example, given that she was the Queen of ancient Britain alongside the renowned King Arthur, we might reasonably expect the legends to furnish her with an appropriately noble parentage and perhaps take the opportunity to offer us a description of the land of her birth. But her family is rarely mentioned (who now remembers her brother Gotegrin or her sisters Lenomie and Floree?[1]) and her mother's existence is barely acknowledged. We are told a little more about her father, who is generally named as Leodegrance, ruler of the remote kingdom of Lyonesse. But he plays a minor role in the legends and once his daughter has been wedded to King Arthur he quickly fades from the scene. All this stands in distinct contrast to the well-documented family history of King Arthur, whose parents Uther PenDragon and Ygrainne were famously assisted by Merlin in the magical mating at Tintagel that led to Arthur's conception.

This same strange absence of information also veils the circumstances surrounding King Arthur's courtship of Gwenevere. We might assume that he would have chosen his bride with an eye to the political or diplomatic advantage that could be gained by marrying the daughter of a neighbouring king, perhaps hoping to forge an alliance that would benefit them both. But there is little suggestion that this was Arthur's motive for choosing Gwenevere, and Leodegrance seems neither to have posed a threat to Arthur nor to have become a friendly ally after the marriage.

If the marriage between Arthur and Gwenevere was not for political reasons, perhaps it was for love? The romance of their courtship would have provided an excellent theme for the storytellers to develop, perhaps elaborating on their first encounter, or describing how Arthur took the opportunity to prove his valour as he plied his suit for Gwenevere's hand and demonstrated his ability to rise to a challenge. This is the stuff of many comparable stories of courtship where the hopeful suitor has to tackle a series of impossible tasks in order to prove his worth. Arthur seems not only to have escaped such trials but does not appear to have put much effort at all into wooing Gwenevere. In fact some sources suggest that rather than going to fetch her himself from her father's kingdom he sent Lancelot to do the job for him. If this is a love story, it falls rather short. Malory describes how when Arthur heard that Gwenevere and the Round Table were about to arrive at his court he was filled with joy at the thought of her arrival and the "rich gift" she was bringing with her.[2] We might be forgiven for wondering if the Round Table, rather than the lady, represented the true object of his desire.

The same air of mystery surrounds Gwenevere's relationship with King Arthur. There is some record of King Arthur's offspring, boys and girls, but the general consensus is that none of these were his children with Gwenevere. Certainly none of them was ever nominated as a possible heir to his throne. It would seem that Gwenevere was unable to bear children and this in itself denies her the more positively defined role that would have been gained through motherhood. This lack of progeny obviously had serious implications for the future of Arthur's line and we might reasonably expect it to be referred to at some point within the stories, but they are curiously and unanimously silent over the matter.

The cumulative effect of these gaps in our knowledge of Gwenevere, far from amounting to nothing, seems on the contrary to amount to something. In our search for Gwenevere's meaning and purpose there appears to be something that we have overlooked, as if we can see the shadow but not the object that causes the shadow.

And here is the key to the mystery, because Gwenevere's name means 'White Shadow'. The element *'wen'*, or *'gwen'* means 'white', 'dazzling', 'holy', and can be found in many early Welsh names. The same element is found in Irish Gaelic, where *finn* or *fionn* means 'white', 'fair'. It is a name frequently given to Faery beings for the simple reason that they can appear to us as dazzling white, shining and fair.

In the precursor to this present study, *Red Tree, White Tree*,[3] I have explored in depth the very real likelihood that Gwenevere is a Faery being, not a human being. When all the evidence for this is brought together and looked at carefully, there can be little doubt that this is so. When we realise that she is a Faery amongst humans, a Faery being living in a human world, we are able to look at the legends from a completely different viewpoint, where rather than perceiving her only as an undistinguished human being we can discover a great deal of positive meaning in her presence as a representative of the Faery race within the court of the Round Table and as a partner to the human King Arthur.

This explains her lack of documented ancestry: Faery 'families' do not conform to the same patterns of father, mother, siblings and clearly defined generations as human families, but are a large, loose-knit group of kindred that changes very little through the passage of time. It also explains Gwenevere's apparent lack of distinctive personality, because Faeries do not possess many of the familiar human characteristics through which we express ourselves on a day to day basis. It explains her lack of progeny: marriages between human and Faery are difficult to sustain on a physical basis and rarely result in offspring. And finally, it explains King Arthur's lack of courtly behaviour in wooing Gwenevere. It is more than likely that the marriage was arranged by Merlin as a means of furthering his initiative to bring the human and Faery races closer together. Neither Arthur nor Gwenevere had very much say in the matter.

Red Tree, White Tree reveals Gwenevere to be a far more powerful and active figure than has previously been realised, a fitting counterpart to King Arthur and a strong presence in the life of the court of the Round Table. In fact it is more accurate to speak of Gwenevere in the present tense: as one of the Faery race she is immortal, and although she has long returned to the world of Faery she is as alive and real for us as she was a thousand years ago if we know where, and how, to find her.

In the mid 20th century the theory emerged that the Arthurian and Grail stories were much more than just a series of romantic and inspiring adventures. It was suggested that they were the memory of a spiritual and magical system which could be traced back to ancient, perhaps even Atlantean, times. This concept was fully developed by Gareth Knight in *The Secret Tradition in Arthurian Legend* in which he demonstrates how the subject matter of the legends falls very convincingly into the traditional structure taught within magical organisations or 'Mystery Schools': three stages of study and progression through the so-called Lesser Mysteries in the court of the Round Table, leading to initiation into the Greater Mysteries, which in the Arthurian legends are revealed in the stories of the Grail.[4]

This means that King Arthur should probably be regarded as one of the ancient line of Sacred Kings, not only an administrator and figurehead to his people but also a Priest, holding the vital link between Deity and the land, maintaining the flow of energy between spirit and matter, in contact with God the Father and Goddess the Mother. In ancient times, the Sacred King's relationship with the Earth Mother was especially maintained through his relationship with a Priestess who was capable of representing the Earth: not only the perfected, sacred aspects of the Earth but all that is as yet imperfect and neglected. In this manner might the Earth be raised through the king's recognition and validation of her hidden sanctity into a Sacred Planet. It was the king's ability to engage in this practice of high magic between the worlds that validated his rulership.

But where in the Arthurian legends can we find the record of this Sacred Kingship? Who is King Arthur's Priestess? If the Arthurian legends are indeed the memory of an ancient and powerful magical system, how was it taught and practiced within the court of the Round Table, and how can the same sacred, magical methods be made relevant to the 21st century?

It is generally agreed that the Round Table was central to King Arthur's court and kingdom, and if nothing else it is certainly an attractive and memorable symbol of equality. It was Gwenevere's dowry, the traditional gift of money or property bestowed upon the husband by the bride's father. But there also exists a faint but persistent belief that the Round Table was Gwenevere's, as if she was associated with it at a level deeper than that of a simple marriage gift.

We can regard the concept of the Round Table on either a literal or a symbolic level, although if we approach it literally it is hard to make much sense of it. The idea of a great wooden table being transported from the distant kingdom of Lyonesse into the court of Camelot where it somehow managed to accommodate upwards of a hundred knights stretches credulity. Why bring a table such a long way? Did Arthur not have a table of his own?

We do better if we look for the symbolic meaning of the Round Table, and viewed in this light it soon speaks to us as a symbol of unity, of fellowship in action, and as a representation of shared purpose at the heart of an organisation where people gather together in their common task. It can also be seen as a symbol of the sphere of the whole earth beneath us, or of the celestial sphere above us, divided into the twelve portions of the solar zodiac and all that they represent.

But while the Round Table represents all these qualities, and it is entirely appropriate that they should be found at the heart of King Arthur's kingdom, it does leave us with the question of why these qualities and this common, universal symbol had to be brought in from elsewhere. Why were they specifically associated with an otherwise unknown ruler of a remote and probably mythical land? What status or authority did Leodegrance possess that qualified him to give such a vital symbol to King Arthur that was soon to become the heart and centre of his rulership? Should we assume that Gwenevere was a mere adjunct to the Round Table, that she happened to come along with it, or did she take a more significant role in its symbolic life within the court?

This book undertakes to answer these questions. It demonstrates how the Round Table was not simply a symbol of equality but was of central, talismanic importance in the work of what was in effect a magical Order of the Round Table. It was central to the court's function as a magical organisation, a School of the Mysteries, and instrumental in the ways in which that magic was revealed, taught and practiced. The magical symbolism of the Round Table was demonstrated and taught by Gwenevere herself: she was the prime interpreter of its wisdom, she worked with its power, and she was responsible for initiating the knights into its Mysteries. The Mysteries of the Round Table were soundly based on an ancient magical wisdom, but over and above this they were specifically concerned with the relationship between Faery and human. The ways in which Gwenevere worked with the power and symbolism of the Round Table are set out clearly in the Arthurian legends, as the following chapters will reveal.

The opening years of the 21st century have seen a surge of interest in the Faery race, witnessed by the increasing desire of many contemporary explorers of the Inner worlds to learn about them and develop a closer relationship with them. It is only in very recent times that the human race has once more begun to open its awareness to the Faeries, but now that the tide has turned, many people are not only acknowledging and accepting their existence but are making conscious and deliberate attempts to move closer to them. The Arthurian legends are full of Faeries! When these stories were first put to paper, humanity's awareness of the immortal race with which it shared the planet was stronger and clearer than it is now. But over the last thousand years the Faery race has gradually slipped away from us; it has faded from our consciousness and its identity has been increasingly misinterpreted. Unfortunately, alongside the increase in our recent understanding of the Faeries has come the popularised and often commercially backed interpretation of them as tiny sprites that wave tinsel wands and flutter their gauzy wings. Nothing could be further from the truth.

The Faeries can teach us a great deal about our world and our place within it, and, paradoxically, they can help us to realise our full potential as human beings. The Faeries' ultimate destiny is irrevocably linked with that of the human race, which means that their capacity to complete the long cycle of their lives on earth and move on, depends to a considerable extent on what they can learn from humanity, what we can learn from them, and how the two races can evolve together. As the physical health of our planet becomes ever more frail, so also does the future of those who inhabit it, Faeries, humans and creatures alike. We have a great deal to learn from each other, not least the means by which we can happily co-exist on the planet that supports our lives.

Like many others of her Faery kind, Gwenevere chose to take on human form and live within the human world in order to bring about a better communication and understanding between the worlds of human and Faery. Within the heart of the kingdom, she acted as a way-shower, building bridges between human and Faery so that others could safely follow and explore for themselves the nature of the Faery race. Gwenevere teaches us how the world looks through Faery eyes. To acquire the ability to see the world as she and her Faery kindred see it is a fascinating and invaluable experience that is without parallel. She also demonstrates to us how the human race appears to the Faeries, and this too, although perhaps a less comfortable experience, brings immense rewards in our ability to understand more of ourselves and our part in the earth's evolution.

But above all, as we look closely at Gwenevere's role within the court of the Round Table, she is revealed as an intelligent, wise, authoritative figure of considerable power. She is not a human being, nor even just a Faery, but a Priestess to the Sacred King, and Initiator to the knights of the Round Table. She taught the magic of the Round Table, and her ability to function in this role is not dimmed by time: she continues to act as Priestess of the Mysteries of the Round Table to all who reach out to her in their imagination.

One of the primary ways in which Gwenevere taught her magic was through the means of the series of apparent 'abductions' that she experienced throughout her life at the court of the Round Table. In *Red Tree, White Tree* it was demonstrated that the most significant pattern in her life was the frequency with which she was 'abducted' from Arthur's court. The outward appearance of these abductions suggests that she was unwillingly captured and taken hostage, but the episodes are far from being a series of calamities. Each time they occurred, one of the knights of the Round Table – usually Gawain or Lancelot, occasionally King Arthur – undertook the challenging journey into the Faery realms in order to retrieve her. Some of these abductions seem to suggest a persistent attempt on the part of her Faery kindred to take her back to themselves, but an equal number reveal a very positive attempt, instigated by Gwenevere herself, to create a series of links or bridges between the human and Faery worlds. Each time she left the human world and returned to Faery, the knight who came to her 'rescue' was led through a series of adventures that challenged him in every aspect. The journeys into Faery thus functioned as a series of lessons in which the knight was educated in the relationship between Faery and human, and the Mysteries of our shared origins and future. These lessons were fundamental to Gwenevere's teaching of the Mysteries of the Round Table.

Although a number of Faery Kingdoms are referred to in the Arthurian legends, Gwenevere is consistently and specifically associated with five of them. These kingdoms are Sorelois, Listenois, Oriande, Gorre and Lyonesse. With the possible exception of Lyonesse they are probably unfamiliar names to most readers, but each kingdom has its own distinct and unique identity, each has a consistent population of Faery characters, and each offers its own challenges, lessons and gifts to those who follow Gwenevere into their Mysteries.

These five Faery lands fall naturally into an archetypal pattern that is found throughout the western magical tradition. It takes the form of a quartered circle about a central point, and thus can represent the cardinal points of the compass, or the daily and yearly cycle of the Sun, or the four elements of air, fire, water and earth about a centre. It is often represented as an equal-armed cross at whose centre blooms a perfect rose. Within the Arthurian legends, Sorelois, Gorre, Lyonesse and Oriande represent the four quarters of the circle or the four points of the cross, while the Grail Kingdom of Listenois lies at its centre. This pattern of five Faery Kingdoms, each closely linked with Gwenevere, lies at the heart of the magical organisation of the Order of the Round Table.

The majority of Faeries who have chosen to incarnate within the human world are female. Many of their stories have been recorded as legend or folk-tale, and their names can be found, for example, in the pages of early Celtic tales where we read of Étaín, Maeve and Fand, or Gwenevere's Irish counterpart Finnabhair. Often a similar pattern is repeated: a female Faery suddenly appears within the human world as if from nowhere and provokes the desire and attention of a human male. More often than not the Faery returns to her own land after a brief period in the human world, leaving her desolate partner to learn, usually the hard way, that many of his previous fantasies about the Faeries were an illusion. But Gwenevere lived in the human world from birth, through childhood and maturity, until her death as a human and her final return into Faery. This puts her in an inimitable position as a mediator between the worlds because she lived through a full range of human experience during her long years as the partner of King Arthur, punctuated only by her regular sojourns in Faery. It is for this reason that she was uniquely able to guide the knights of the Round Table, and now ourselves, in a variety of different approaches to her own Faery reality.

As counterpart to Gwenevere, King Arthur represents the voice of humanity. Sadly, one of his main functions within the magical Order of the Round Table seems to have been to demonstrate humanity's attitude in general towards Faery that, it has to be said, leaves much to be desired. The loud, hasty and aggressive ways of humankind leave little time for the delicate music of Faery. The question of communication and understanding between Faery and human did not appear to concern King Arthur overmuch, certainly not the Arthur who is portrayed in the legends. A real and lasting relationship with Faery inevitably goes hand in hand with new and challenging realisations about our own selves, and the Once and Future King must one day be at the forefront of our relationship with Faery.

The following chapters offer the reader a variety of practical experiences of the work of the magical Order of the Round Table as it was taught and initiated by Gwenevere. Much of the theory behind this magical work is discussed in *Red Tree, White Tree* and you may find it useful to acquire this background of knowledge before you begin to work with it in practice. However, the present book is complete in itself. It contains a series of meditations, guided visualisations and magical journeys into the lands of Faery, each led by Gwenevere, and each based on material that is readily found in the legends themselves. Together with the many challenges this magical work will present to you, you will discover a light, life and joy which have the power to transform your own life and, step by step, will serve to bring the human and Faery worlds a little closer. Ultimately, the Faeries can show us the highest levels of creation where we may walk with the angels.

As Seekers of the eternal wisdom of the Inner worlds, the knights of the Round Table were taught the knowledge and understanding of the patterns of the universe, they were trained to develop their skills in entering the Inner worlds, and they were shown how to work in harmony with the universal energies that run between the starry worlds above and the dragons of the Inner earth below. Above all, as Initiates of the Mysteries of the Round Table, they were taught how to communicate with the immortal race of Faery, to safely explore the Faery kingdoms, and to relate to the Star Goddess beloved by the Faery race. So also, by working through the material in the following pages, may you become an Initiate of these Mysteries.

All of the magical work that follows can be practiced equally successfully whether you are working on your own, with a partner, or within a group. At each stage of the way you will be guided by Gwenevere. You will find her a wise and joyful companion, and a skilled and loving initiator into the Mysteries of the Round Table.

1   They are mentioned in Heinrich von dem Türlin, *Diu Crône*, ed. G.H.F. Scholl (Stuttgart: Bibliothek de Littevarischenvereins, Vol XXVIII, 1852)
2   Thomas Malory, *Le Morte D'Arthur*, ed. Janet Cowen (London: Penguin Books, 1969)
3   Wendy Berg, *Red Tree, White Tree*, (Cheltenham: Skylight Press, 2010)
4   Gareth Knight, *The Secret Tradition in Arthurian Legend* (York Beach: Weiser, 1996)

CHAPTER TWO

The Mysteries of the Round Table

BEFORE WE LOOK AT how the Mysteries of the Round Table were taught and practiced, we need to acquire a working knowledge of the principles on which they were based. It is often assumed that the Round Table made its first appearance as if from nowhere at the time of King Arthur's marriage to Gwenevere, but in fact it had already accumulated quite a history before it finally made its way to his court. It is described throughout the earlier versions of the Arthurian legends and was associated with no less than five previous owners. Each inheritor of the Round Table and the magical Order associated with it built on what had gone before, so that Gwenevere's comparatively late connection with it not only marked the highest point of its achievement but placed her in a perfect position to interpret its meaning. And, as we shall explore in later chapters, its work continued after her death and remains vitally relevant to the present day.

The earliest known reference to the Round Table is found in the chronicles of the Anglo-Norman Wace, who was born in Jersey *c.*1110. His *History of the British* was completed around 1155 and is based on Geoffrey of Monmouth's *History of the Kings of Britain*. But while Geoffrey does not mention the Round Table at all, Wace makes quite a feature of it and is unique in contributing its construction to King Arthur himself. He tells how Arthur was troubled by the dissent that had broken out among his ambitious barons, and had come up with the idea of seating them about a round table as a means of keeping the peace when they were gathered together in his dining hall. In this new arrangement everyone was equal, there were no leaders, and nobody was served with the best food before the others in the customary deference to their rank.[1]

This model of the Round Table as a symbol of equality where all are treated with impartiality, and where there are no leaders or hierarchy, has proved to be its most enduring image. Indeed, the very concept of a round table has become synonymous with these qualities of fellowship, discussion and concord, the perfect symbol of a meeting place where disagreement and dissent can be resolved. A circular table makes a strong and positive image: it is a softer, more approachable shape than a square or rectangle, whether it is used as a dining table, a seating arrangement in a conference hall or as any symbolic representation of unity and wholeness.

Wace takes the pragmatic view that Arthur constructed the table simply as a means to this end, a practical solution to his problem of keeping the peace within a group of strong-minded individuals rather than the symbolic expression of a higher ideal or the symbol of a chivalrous order of knighthood. His is a purely secular interpretation: there is little in Wace of the deeper symbolism that imbues the later narratives, and nothing at all of the quest for the Grail which soon, and suddenly, would become such a driving force in the Arthurian mythos. If Wace was aware of the deeper meaning behind the life and times of King Arthur, as is possible, he chose not to make it part of his narrative.

However, this earliest account of the Round Table does provide us with the vital foundation that underpins everything that would later be built upon these bare bones. Without this fundamental expression of unity and harmony at the heart of the court of the Round Table, all that it later came to symbolise would be built on unstable ground. The very ethos of the Round Table is one of mutual respect and equality and if it lacks this basis it comes to nothing, even though the concept is deeper in its implications than Wace might have realised.

Wace was closely followed by Lawman,[2] a priest and scribe who lived and worked in what is now the county of Worcestershire near the River Severn in England. He translated Wace's work into English and added several significant elements not found in the earlier work. In what is perhaps his most notable addition, Lawman describes how one Christmastide King Arthur invited ambassadors from all the countries he had subdued – Scotland, Ireland and Iceland to name but a few – to join him in the festivities. Things didn't go entirely to plan because no sooner had they all gathered together in the dining hall than fierce rivalry for position broke out amongst them. The dispute began as a verbal disagreement, escalated into a free-for-all with bread and goblets of wine flying through the air, rapidly degenerated into a full scale fight, initially with blows and punches but then with swords, and culminated in a bloodbath. King Arthur had a riot on his hands instead of Christmas lunch. He subdued it by carrying out a swift and severe punishment on the men responsible *and* their wives and relations who, he said, would be treated as traitors if such unruliness ever happened again.[3] Peace was restored, but one cannot help thinking that his reaction was a little severe. Perhaps the episode is the memory of a greater, more ancient conflict? Lawman doesn't give us sufficient information to be certain, but the episode seems to hint at more than meets the eye.

Lawman then describes how, soon after this incident, King Arthur visited Cornwall where he was approached by a mysterious and unidentified man. The stranger told him that news of the fight had reached him overseas! As soon as he had heard of the *fracas,* he told Arthur, he had returned to England to help him prevent such disorder happening again. He suggested that Arthur might benefit from the fact that he was capable of some marvellously skilled woodwork, and offered to make him a table where all his men could sit together as equals. This table, he declared, would not only easily seat upwards of sixteen hundred knights but whenever Arthur wanted to ride out from the court or travel about his kingdom it could be folded away and carried on horseback, ready to be set up again wherever it was needed! Arthur understandably found this an attractive proposition, and the mystery man had the table constructed and ready for use within a month.

A table that can seat over sixteen hundred knights yet also be packed into a bag and carried on horseback can be no ordinary piece of furniture. In fact it is hard to be certain what this 'table' actually looked like, and Lawman's description of it is not clear. The only unambiguous way to describe a round table is to call it just that, but Lawman says rather circumspectly that it will enable the knights to be seated in turn, so that no-one was either included or excluded, but that each man would be seated opposite another.[4] It sounds almost as if a *circle* of tables is being described, with the knights seated on both the inside and outside. And yet, if the table was small enough to carry on horseback it can only have seated Arthur and a couple of other men at the most. The only interpretation that makes any sense is that Lawman is describing two completely different things, neither of which sounds very much like a round table! And yet it is evident that something of great significance has been introduced into Arthur's court.

Lawman's other main departure from Wace is to reject the suggestion that the table was made by Arthur himself and to introduce the mysterious man of knowledge from overseas who had heard of Arthur's difficulties, sought him out in his moment of need and offered him some practical help and effective advice. This man must surely be more than a simple carpenter. His timely appearance so soon after a major crisis, his surprising knowledge of Arthur's current circumstances, even from abroad, and his ability to initiate a radical change of direction at the heart of Arthur's court all suggest that this is likely to be none other than Merlin himself. If this is so, we might guess that he had not been 'abroad' at all but had made one of his regular reappearances from the Inner worlds just when he was needed. We can readily bring to mind other examples of his ability to do this, perhaps none so striking as the occasion on which Arthur broke his first sword and Merlin guided him to the Lady of the Lake who was able to provide him with a new one.

Another clue to the man's identity might be found in his claim to possess marvellous skills as a woodworker, although perhaps this is not something we would normally associate with Merlin. The phrase brings to mind the ancient magical game of *fidchell* or 'wood sense' played by the kings and heroes of Irish and Welsh mythology, where a chequered gaming board was a practical magical tool that came into life when played upon, as if it stood between the outer and Inner worlds.[5] The term 'wood sense' referred not so much to the skills of carpentry involved in making the board but to the power of the board and the magical skills required of its players as they moved the symbolic pieces about its surface. In *The Dream of Rhonabwy*, a tale in the *Mabinogion*, King Arthur plays the game with Owein, using golden men on a silver board. In *The Dream of Macsen Wledig*, Eudaf Hen carves the pieces for his own golden board.[6] Gwenevere also plays this magical game, seated at a crossroads in a forest that lies between the human and Faery worlds – a neglected but highly significant episode in the journey towards the Faery Kingdom of Listenois that will be explored in a later chapter.

Whatever the identity of King Arthur's mysterious advisor, there can be little doubt that what he gave to Arthur in order to bring peace and harmony to his troubled court was, as Lawman suggests, two very different things. The first of these was a small, magical chequered gameboard that was perhaps set in a wooden round, something that Arthur could keep close by him when he was at his court *and* when he moved about the country. Because this magical artefact was especially made by the mysterious stranger in response to the problems at Arthur's court, it seems very likely that it was not just a piece of furniture but a symbolic, talismanic representation of a powerful Innerworld concept that was capable of addressing at a deep level the underlying reasons for the discord. This wooden talisman was not for general public use or display but would only have been used by those who had the Inner knowledge and skill to enable them to use such a powerful magical symbol responsibly.

Separate to this mysterious object, a new seating arrangement seems to have been introduced at the same time within Arthur's court, which enabled him and his company of men to come together in unity and equality by sitting in a circle. This arrangement was obviously linked to the magical talisman, but was an outerworld expression of the Inner, universal principles the talisman represented.

In effect, Lawman is giving a concise description of the exoteric and esoteric aspects of a system of Inner Wisdom. What was actually given to Arthur, and we may assume that it was given to him by Merlin, was the revelation of this wisdom in a form which would provide the basis of a magical Order that was to become established, under Merlin's guidance, within Arthur's court. The symbolic heart of this organisation was a magical artefact of a size that could easily be carried. The magical knowledge it represented would be studied and practiced by Arthur and those of his knights who were initiated into its secrets. Among the many transformational effects that would be experienced by those who studied its wisdom, the most immediately obvious was the change in behaviour from aggressive power struggle to peace and harmony that was brought about in Arthur's men. An alternative seating arrangement at dinner is not usually sufficient in itself to achieve such a fundamental change of behaviour in a group of rivals!

Lawman makes no further mention of the table's attributes, but the connection between a circular table at which all may sit in equality, and a talismanic representation of a system of Inner Wisdom introduced by Merlin into Arthur's court, has been established. As to the nature or tradition of this system of wisdom Lawman has no more to tell us, although those who followed him had plenty to say on the matter.

At the end of the 12th century, 40 years after Wace and Lawman, and some 20 years after Chrétien de Troyes had produced his highly influential *Percevale,* Robert de Boron wrote his *Joseph of Arimathea* and *Merlin.*[7] In these stories, he makes a clear link between the Round Table and the Grail. We are now so familiar with the idea that a connection exists between them that we tend not to question how it came about, but Boron is the first known writer to have made this link, and his additions to the range and depth of the Round Table's symbolism take us forward in leaps and bounds

Much of Boron's narrative is told through the voice of Merlin, a literary and magical masterstroke which succeeds not only in bringing together the two apparently disparate elements of early Christian esoteric history and British pagan mythology, but at the same time imbues them with a magical *gravitas* such as can only come from the mouth of the Arch Mage of Britain himself. In Boron's narrative, Merlin is again said to be responsible for constructing the Round Table, although not for King Arthur but his father Uther PenDragon.

Merlin describes the history and symbolism of the Round Table to Uther PenDragon at considerable length before he hands it over to him, and is at pains to emphasise that the table's symbolism and meaning will only be fully understood when its previous history has also been understood. This is a vitally important point, although it tends to be overlooked. In fact, Merlin tells Uther, the present table is the last in a line of *three* Round Tables, and his description of the meaning of these three tables takes up a considerable portion of the narrative.

Merlin begins by tracing the Round Table's history backwards in time in order to explain how the Grail was actually the vessel used by Christ at the Last Supper. The table at which this meal was shared, Merlin says, constituted the first Round Table. This same sacred vessel, Merlin tells Uther, was then used by Joseph of Arimathea to receive Christ's blood after the crucifixion.

Merlin continues by describing how after the death and resurrection of Christ, Joseph of Arimathea left the Holy Land and survived a forty-year imprisonment, during which he was sustained only by the power of the sacred vessel. After his release, he travelled for some years with a group of people that included several members of his own family. At a critical point in their journey he revealed the Grail to his companions, an action that produced striking results but which also marked the end of their journey together and initiated a new stage in the Grail's history. The table on which Joseph placed the Grail when he first revealed it to his company was the second Round Table. Soon after this revelation of the Grail, a group of twelve emerged from the larger company. These twelve became the guardians of the Grail and were eventually responsible for bringing it to Avalon, in Britain.

Finally, Merlin roots these past events into the Arthurian mythos and into the very land of Britain by creating the third Round Table, for Uther PenDragon, which incorporated the symbolism and meaning of the two previous tables – the table of the Last Supper and the table made by Joseph of Arimathea. Merlin tells Uther that this third table should be kept in Uther's castle of Caerdoel, where he, Merlin, will choose fifty men to be seated around it. When they take their places, Merlin promises, they will never want to leave it or return to their homes, and Uther will finally be able to understand the full significance of all three Round Tables.

One of the greatest subtleties of Boron's remarkable story is that although he claims to be describing the significance of actual physical tables, what he is actually describing, in veiled language, is the hidden knowledge and system of Inner wisdom that these tables represent, and the secrets of those who have been initiated into this wisdom. There is an allegorical quality to his prose that places the outward events of the story beyond their apparent time and place, while the very simplicity and matter-of-factness of his writing belies the extraordinary nature of what he is actually revealing to his readers. There is a great deal to be found hidden beneath the surface of Boron's text, none more so than in the precise detailing of the sequence and nature of the events that takes place between the Last Supper and the arrival of the Grail in Britain.

Merlin tells Uther that after Christ's Resurrection, Joseph was imprisoned in a tower for forty years, during which time he was sustained only by the powers contained within the sacred vessel which filled him with a spiritual sustenance of such power that he was transformed from his physical body into a Being of Light. This sacred vessel, we remember, was not only the receptacle of the wine that represented Christ's blood at the Last Supper but also contained some of Christ's actual blood taken by Joseph of Arimathea after the crucifixion. Joseph was eventually released from prison by Vespasian, the son of the Emperor Titus. When Vespasian lifted the stone slab which sealed the prison, he could at first see only a brilliant white light that completely filled the tower's interior.

Following his release, Joseph left the Holy Land with a selected group of people and lived with them for some time in an unnamed country. During this period, they lived off the land, supporting themselves by growing all that they needed. But after an initial period of abundance, the fertility of the land declined until it ceased to provide for their needs and they were faced with starvation. They pleaded with Joseph to help them discover what was going wrong, and by way of an answer he created a table in memory of the table of the Last Supper. He placed the sacred vessel on the table and covered it in a white cloth. Next to the vessel, he placed a fish that had been caught by his sister's husband, Bron. Many of his company were able to sit at the table, but some of them were not able to do so, although it is not stated why they could not. Those who were able to sit at the table were also able to see the sacred vessel, and these same people found within it the fulfilment of their heart's desire. The others, even though they were standing nearby, were not able to see the sacred vessel and were not able to experience its powers of fulfilment.

It was said that this latter group of people was responsible for causing the failure of the land, and it was explained to them that the Grail's powers had revealed this difference between the two groups.

Some time afterwards, a group of twelve men emerged from the company. They were said to be the twelve sons of Joseph's sister Enigeus. The group was led by her husband Bron, who was known as the Fisher King. The title, which was from then on closely associated with the guardians of the Grail, must surely refer to a role of authority within an esoteric tradition rather than suggest that he was an actual fisherman: fishermen aren't usually described as Kings.[8] Inevitably a comparison can be made between this group of twelve and the twelve disciples, although Boron doesn't make this overt connection. This group became responsible for the guardianship of the sacred vessel, which was now known as the Grail, and took it westwards into the hidden vales of Avalon where it was withdrawn from human sight. Avalon, it is worth reminding ourselves, is an Inner, Faery realm closely linked to the physical landscape around Glastonbury.

In concluding his story, Merlin makes a final and very important comment concerning the Grail's continuing significance after its withdrawal into the Inner worlds. After demonstrating the exact nature of its powers, the Grail was then guarded by the Fisher King and his successors within the Faery realms until such time as it should be rediscovered by a questing knight who was able to understand the meaning of what he had discovered. Merlin says that when, in the future, a knight from Arthur's court should find the hidden castle of the Fisher King, he should ask what purpose the Grail *had served.*

The importance of the use of the past tense can hardly be over-emphasised. Through the voice of Merlin, Boron is telling the reader quite plainly that the key to understanding the Grail can be found in its history, in the very story that he has set out in his narrative. It is perfectly clear whom the Grail has served: it has served Joseph of Arimathea, by bringing about a transformation within him from physical body to Body of Light and providing the means whereby he could continue to live without actual nourishment. Through the powers of the Grail, he had been transformed from a mortal human inhabiting a physical body into an immortal being of light. This is the purpose that the Grail had served. Boron does not use the word Faery (in fact the word is almost never used in the Arthurian and Grail mythos) but that should not deter us from making this connection ourselves. As Merlin is at pains to point out to Uther PenDragon, this very power of the Grail was a vital part of the Round Table's symbolism and significance.

Another significant point in Merlin's narrative is that although Joseph's companions started out as a single group, after a while they separated into two factions. Merlin describes how the Grail also served to indicate the fundamental difference between them: one group of people could see the Grail and benefit from it just as Joseph had done while he was imprisoned in the tower. The other group could not see or benefit from the Grail, and this group was linked to the estrangement that had occurred between the people and the land, and with the land's loss of fertility.

Boron's lack of reference to location of the land in which these seminal events took place enables it to take on a symbolic quality, and the story can be read as a parable of the ancient history of the two races of Faery and human. The two races lived together in harmony for a while but their differences became more pronounced, until the point of crisis was reached and a seemingly irrevocable rift occurred, often described as the 'Fall'. Those of the human race gradually lost their intimate connection with the land, with disastrous consequences. This same concept of the failed land took on an increasingly important role in the Arthurian and Grail legends where it became known as the Waste Land. The healing of the Waste Land was dependent on the Grail Seeker's ability to understand the meaning of the history of the Grail.

The means by which the sacred vessel revealed the source of this problem is consistent with what Merlin tells us of its powers. It was able to sustain some of those in Joseph's company with a supra-physical nourishment such as it had already done for Joseph during his imprisonment. Only those who were able to perceive and comprehend its existence on the higher planes of creation were able to benefit from it, and we must assume that they could do so because they were themselves existing at that higher level of vibration. Those of the human race could not see the Grail even though they were standing right next to it, because it no longer had a physical form. The transformational powers of the Grail were of course not a property of the physical vessel or the table on which it was placed, but on the transforming power of Christ's blood which it contained.

The "deep secret" that Merlin reveals to Uther PenDragon (and later to King Arthur) concerns the body of esoteric knowledge that the outward symbol of the table represents, particularly in its connection with the Grail. The entire purpose of Merlin's explanation of its history is that Uther, and all subsequent initiates in the Mysteries of the Round Table, would be in full possession of this magical symbolism. This is entirely in accordance with what we learnt from Lawman, where the 'Round Table' is a synonym for a system of magical knowledge and practice.

According to Merlin, the significance of the Grail's powers is intimately connected to both the human and Faery races. We can see a parallel between the division that was revealed in Joseph's followers when they gathered about his Round Table, and the division that occurred within Arthur's men which was healed by the instigation of the Round Table. The Grail has significance not only in regard to the separation that occurred between these two races but also provides the means by which that division may be healed in the future. But this will only come about when the entire history of the Round Table's symbolism is understood and worked with in practice, and this constitutes a vital part of the magical work of the Order of the Round Table.

However, as Merlin explains to Uther PenDragon, these Mysteries of the Grail are not the only Mysteries connected with the Round Table. It is only when the Grail Mysteries are conjoined with the ancient system of wisdom that had already been established by Merlin within the court of Uther PenDragon, that their full significance will be understood.

But the Round Table had yet to pass from Uther PenDragon to Arthur, and many years passed between Uther's death and Arthur's marriage to Gwenevere. The final link in the chain is provided by one of the later Arthurian romances, the 'Vulgate Cycle', a series of five works written by an anonymous author or group of authors c.1225.[9] The first part of this extensive work repeats and elaborates the early history of the Grail as told by Boron, but later chapters focus on Merlin's role in Arthur's conception and birth, and the establishment of his kingdom. Much of this section is devoted to interminable descriptions of Arthur's battles with the Saxons and sundry other marauders but one of these encounters provides the vital link with Gwenevere.

The episode describes how Merlin, after the death of Uther PenDragon, took the Round Table from Uther's court at Caerdoel and placed it in the keeping of Gwenevere's father, King Leodegrance of Carmelide (an alternative name for Lyonesse). At this point in the story Leodegrance is an old man, and Gwenevere is expected soon to inherit his kingdom. Carmelide was under constant threat from a certain King Rion, king of the Land of Giants and Pastures.[10] Arthur rides to the court of Leodegrance at the city of Carhaix in Carmelide, accompanied by Merlin and forty men. They engage in battle with Rion and his giants, and after many skirmishes including an episode in which Arthur rescues Leodegrance from certain death at Rion's hands, Rion and his giants are eventually overpowered. Their defeat, it has to be said, is almost entirely due to Merlin's power over the elements. During the course of the battle he raises a whirlwind that collapses the tents on the heads of Rion's men, raises a cloud of dust so that the combatants can't see each other, and then transforms the dragon on his banner into a flame-thrower that scorches anyone or anything that gets in his way. A useful man to have on your side.

Following the defeat of Rion, Leodegrance happily agrees that his daughter Gwenevere should marry Arthur. As we know, Leodegrance then gave his Round Table to King Arthur as Gwenevere's marriage dowry. But what especially interests us in this episode is that not only did the Round Table belong to Leodegrance but so also did an elite group of knights especially associated with it: the Knights of the Round Table. According to the Vulgate Cycle they formed a distinct group within Leodegrance's army and in fact are often referred to as 'companions' rather than knights, implying that the bond between them was more than that of a fighting force. It is clear that after the death of Uther PenDragon, not only the Round Table but the whole magical system connected with it had been given to Leodegrance. So, in turn, Arthur not only inherited the outer symbol of the Round Table but also the group of knights who had been initiated into its Mysteries, and the body of teaching that went with it. No wonder he was pleased!

The Vulgate Cycle devotes only a paragraph to this event and barely pauses to take breath before resuming its interminable tally of battles. But we must pause to consider the significance of what the authors of the Vulgate Cycle so briefly gloss over. Why was the Round Table given to a previously unknown character, Leodegrance, after the death of Uther PenDragon? If the Round Table, both as a symbolic object and as an esoteric Order, had needed a home in the years between Uther and Arthur when Logres lacked a king, why did Merlin choose an otherwise unheard of individual who apart from his connection with Gwenevere plays almost no part in the story? Why didn't Merlin himself, as instigator of the Mysteries of the Round Table, resume temporary guardianship?

If we lacked the knowledge of Gwenevere's Faery identity, Merlin's choice of Leodegrance as guardian of the Round Table would make no sense. But with the benefit of the knowledge that Gwenevere, and therefore her father, are of the Faery race, we can see that this episode in the Round Table's history provides the final link in its thread of meaning. The Mysteries of the Round Table are especially concerned with the relationship between human and Faery and so it makes perfect sense that before they were finally established in the court of King Arthur they should spend a period of time under Faery guardianship. We can assume therefore that the companions of the Round Table in Leodegrance's court were a combination of previously initiated knights of the Round Table from Uther PenDragon's court and Leodegrance's own Faery Warriors who had become members of the same Inner Order. Their new oath of allegiance to King Arthur signalled the arrival of a significant company of knights of Faery into his court, something which is often overlooked.

But even more significantly, they arrived with one of their own kindred, Gwenevere, who as the daughter of one of the Round Table's principle guardians and the inheritor of its Mysteries was uniquely qualified to teach its wisdom.

Before we explore and experience how she achieved this, it is worth keeping in mind the many levels of meaning she was working with.

On both an immediate level, and at a deeper level, the Round Table is an expression of equality and unity in a shared goal.

It is a representation of the Solar Cross of Atlantean magic: a quartered circle about a central point. This symbol was later expressed as the Rose Cross, the perfect rose that blooms at the centre when the four elements are brought back into balance and harmony within the earth. This ancient basis of magical wisdom was first established and taught by Merlin, within the court of Uther PenDragon.

Later, during the time of King Arthur, this pattern was expressed in the division of ancient Britain into the four lands of Logres, Gales, Hibernia and Caledonia about the central point of Camelot. In the Faery realms, the four lands were Lyonesse, Sorelois, Gorre and Oriande about the central kingdom of Listenois, the Grail kingdom.

Onto this basis of the quartered circle, or equal-armed cross, was then introduced the means by which the ancient division and separation between Faery and human could be explored, understood and resolved. This was achieved by Gwenevere's example in her marriage to King Arthur, through her guidance and tuition, and through her creation of opportunities to learn about the Faery race, to travel into their world, and to discover how to relate to them.

Finally, as the culmination to this work, the Christian Mysteries were introduced into the Order of the Round Table. Not the exoteric Christianity of the Church but the esoteric Christianity revealed within the story of Joseph of Arimathea and the journey of the Grail from the Holy Land into the Faery realms of Britain.

It was Gwenevere's task to guide and initiate the knights through the magical work of the Order of the Round Table, leading them towards an ultimate realisation of the Mysteries of the Grail. In the following chapters you will be shown how she did this, and you will discover how to experience this magic for yourself.

1 Wace and Lawman, *The Life of King Arthur* trans. Judith Weiss (London, Everyman Paperback, 1997) p.51

2 His name can also be written as Layamon.

3 Ibid, p.240

4 Ibid, p.241

5 The Welsh version is known as Gwyddbwylch.

6 Gwyn Jones and Thomas Jones, trans., *The Mabinogion* (London: Dent, 1974)

7 Robert de Boron, *Merlin and the Grail: Joseph of Arimathea, Merlin, Perceval,* trans. Nigel Bryant (Cambridge, D.S. Brewer, 2001)

8 The name 'Bron' has been likened to 'Bran' of Celtic mythology, but the similarity between 'Bron' and 'Boron' is equally persuasive! If 'Fisher King' is indeed an esoteric title of authority, one can't help but speculate that it might have been held by Boron.

9 Norris J. Lacy, general editor, *Lancelot-Grail: The old French Arthurian Vulgate and Post-Vulgate in translation* (New York and London, Garland Publishing Inc., 1993)

10 King Rion appears in various guises throughout the Arthurian chronicles but is always a giant, often described as wearing armour decorated with crowns and sheaves of grain, and the possessor of a magical sword called Marmiadoise that had once been owned by Hercules. His kingdom, which lies further west than Carmelide, is filled with such strange happenings that nobody dares to live there.

CHAPTER THREE

How to see Faeries

URING THE PERIOD in which Joseph of Arimathea travelled with the sacred vessel of the Grail in its journey from Jerusalem to Avalon, the group that accompanied him gradually separated into two factions. One of the main indications of the difference between the two groups was that those in one group could see the Grail and benefit from its powers of sustenance, but those in the other could not. It was claimed that the inability of those in the second group to see the Grail was the due to their uncontrolled lust, and that the main function of the Grail was to separate the 'good' from the 'bad'. This specious morality is oddly persuasive: the idea that only the virtuous and pure can see the Grail has become widely accepted, but the accumulation of guilt, blame and feelings of inadequacy it has fostered, has paralysed the quest of many Grail Seekers.

We need to set this aside once and for all. If the separation between the good and the bad was really the sacred vessel's prime purpose this would place it at complete odds with the ethos of the Communion with Christ in which *all* are invited to partake for spiritual renewal. If we remove this hollow morality from the story we are left with a pragmatic and much more useful explanation. The inability of some of Joseph's company to see the Grail was simply because it existed at a higher level of vibration than the physical world. This is, after all, one of the main reasons why we can't see things!

Our ability to see the Grail depends largely on our ability to perceive the subtle forms of the Inner planes, and this especially includes the forms of the Faery beings who inhabit the worlds just beyond our own. As with any School of the Mysteries, the practical magical work of the Round Table begins with the development of the student's ability to perceive and recognise the forms of the Inner worlds, and this chapter provides you with a variety of exercises specifically designed to that purpose. If you feel confident in your ability to see the Faeries, you may wish to pass straight on to the next chapter. But most people will find something of use and interest in the following exercises, and you can dip into them and return to them whenever you feel the need.

Most of us are unable to see Faeries with our normal, everyday vision. This is because they inhabit a world that exists at a slightly higher level of vibration than that of our own physical world and is therefore just beyond our normal range of perception. Faeries have 'bodies' in the sense that they tend to maintain something of a recognisably consistent appearance, but their bodies are much less fixed and solid than our own. They are formed of shining light and colour, and only a little of this light and colour passes through into the material world we inhabit. But with practice, it is easy to increase your ability to perceive them and the Inner worlds they inhabit.

It is good to keep in mind right from the start that communicating with Gwenevere and her Faery kindred is a two-way process that in many respects works just like any communication between two humans. If you are doubtful or half-hearted in your belief in the existence of Faeries they will quite understandably be less than enthusiastic in trying to communicate with you! On the other hand if you show a genuine desire to learn more about them and are wholehearted in your approach, they will often respond by stepping down their level of vibration in order to come closer to you, just as you will be raising your level of consciousness in order to move closer to them.

Generally speaking, the nearest that the Faeries come to our world is the level just beyond that of physical matter that is often referred to as the etheric level, which is quite closely linked to the physical. The light that shines through the Faeries' bodies can easily be glimpsed under the right conditions. Folk tradition maintains that the Faeries don't like us to look straight at them, and there is some truth in this. If you try to see them by looking straight at them you will make things more difficult for yourself because you will not be using the most light-sensitive part of your eye. The centre of the eye contains a larger proportion of the nerves that are used for detecting detail, but the periphery of the eye contains nerves which are more sensitive to light. So if you try to catch sight of the Faeries through the corner of your eye rather than looking straight at them, you will better be able to detect the light and colour of their bodies that shines through the veil into our physical world.

When you are learning how to develop your relationship with the Faeries and increase your ability to communicate with them, set aside regular periods for walking in natural surroundings such as woodlands during the day, and remember to look up at the stars at night. In this way you will begin to build a bridge in your consciousness between the physical world of humanity and the Inner world of Faery.

The best place to practice this first exercise is when you are out walking in an environment such as the dappled light and shade of woodland that is the Faeries' natural home. Walking amongst trees, send out your desire to see the Faeries, quietly assure them of your sincere wish to get to know them, and then place your attention at the periphery of your vision as you walk. The trick is to *soften* your vision and allow the muscles around your eyes to relax, avoiding direct, focused attention on any of the details of your surroundings. Let your gaze rest gently on the mid-distance. After a while you may become aware of occasional faint movements of light and shadow at the corners of your eyes, and perhaps begin to glimpse the Faery forms.

'Seeing' Faeries is actually more a matter of sensing, or intuiting, or knowing, rather than actually seeing them as you would with your normal everyday sight. This type of looking at things on the Inner levels of creation is very different to the narrow range of vision we normally adopt when dealing with the physical world. The world about us demands our focused perception, and this blocks out the subtle energies that lie behind the material forms. When you begin to withdraw your focus of vision from the physical world you simultaneously also heighten your consciousness just a little so that in effect you are entering a slight dreaminess, or a gentle meditative state.

Developing your Inner vision and increasing your sensitivity to the light and colour of the worlds that lie beyond the physical plane is a technique well worth practising when you are approaching the Inner worlds in general, but especially useful for perceiving the Faeries. You need not work through the following exercises all at once; they should be taken one at a time and you can return to them as you progress through the book. It is suggested that you begin by practicing each exercise out of doors whenever possible, and then follow this up by working through the exercise again, indoors, in meditation.

DEVELOPING SENSITIVITY TO FAERY LIGHT AND COLOUR

You will of course be familiar with the seven colours of the rainbow, the visible spectrum of red, orange, yellow, green, blue, indigo and violet. When you see a rainbow arching over the sky, especially when it is set against a backdrop of dark thunder-clouds, its colours are far more delicately beautiful than those which you see around you in the mundane world. These light-infused colours of the rainbow are nearer to the quality of Faery colours than the colours of the everyday world, but true Faery colours are even more beautiful.

The following exercises should be worked through one colour at a time, and one step at a time. Ideally, it's best to start with red, and progress through orange, yellow and green in turn. (The colours blue, indigo and violet form part of the more advanced work in a later chapter.) But if there are practical reasons why this is not possible, be flexible. For example, the exercises for perceiving Faery orange ask you to find some orange flowers in bloom. If you have begun to read this book in winter and are unable to find any orange flowers, move on to the next colour and return to orange when you can.

As with any acquired skill, frequent and regular short efforts will work best. Long sessions separated by long intervals will not work so well. Each exercise should only take ten minutes or so, and indeed it is better not to take much longer than this to start with, as you will become tired and lose concentration.

Another vital part of your work with the Faeries is that you should keep a record of all your thoughts and realisations, and it will help you to treasure what you are achieving if you make your record look attractive. The reason why it is important to keep a record of your work is that much of it lies between the Inner and outer worlds and on the borders of your everyday consciousness, so it will soon slip away once you return to the outer world. Just as a dream quickly fades from conscious memory when you wake up and start your day, so will much of your work with Faery be lost to your conscious mind unless you write it down. It will also give you encouragement to look back at what you have written and realise how much you have learnt and discovered since you started. Record your meditation results, your dreams, your realisations, intuitions and thoughts.

Remember that you are not only working at developing your perception of the Faeries' world of light and colour but you are also now starting to form a relationship with those of the Faery race who will be working with you as you take your place at the Round Table. You are beginning the process of opening a two-way channel of communication, and every time you work with these exercises in meditation you will be sending out a signal to the Faeries that you are trying to contact them. The more regularly you practice, the more readily they will tune in to you and begin to work with you. It will help this two-way process if you try to meditate at the same time each day, and preferably in the same place, whether this is indoors in your meditation space or a specially chosen spot out of doors.

You might like to begin each meditation by lighting a candle (if you are working indoors) and by voicing a short phrase of aspiration. For example: 'My intention is to open a gateway of communication with the Faeries, for the benefit of all who inhabit the earth.'

WORKING WITH FAERY RED

A true, pure red is rarely seen in the western world. Its warming, sensual, energising quality can be used to great effect, but because red is associated with the human attributes of sexuality, anger and fear it is closely associated with the expression of that part of the human life-force which is manifested through the human root chakra which Faeries do not possess. These three qualities are the main components of the human 'shadow' and are therefore rarely experienced by the Faeries. Red is the colour of human blood, and this brings us to a fundamental point of difference between humans and Faeries. Faery 'blood,' in the sense of the life-force which supports them, is not red but composed of a shining translucency whose colour is best described as a dazzling white.

For these reasons, red is found only in certain special circumstances in the Faery world. Red lies at the bottom end of the visible spectrum and is rarely adopted by them; they cannot tolerate it in large doses. But when the Faeries make a deliberate effort to become visible to us it is quite likely that they will step down their rate of vibration by adopting an article of clothing such as red shoes or a red hat which is more easily visible to us. This is why the colour red is most commonly used by the goblins, pixies and other small Faery creatures who live comparatively near to the earth, and by those Faery characters who have a particularly rumbustious nature. It is rarely used by the higher Faeries such as Gwenevere or her kindred because they exist at a higher rate of vibration than the elemental Faeries and gnomes. But for the first attempts to perceive Inner colours, red is the ideal place to start.

Read through all six steps of the following exercise, then work through them one at a time.

1. Your first step towards awareness of red in the Faeries' world comes by opening your awareness to the many different reds that you can see about you in the physical world. During the day, as you travel to work or sit in your garden, observe the vast range of different reds around you. They will vary from muddy shades of rusty brown and dull crimson, through bright scarlet, to the harshly glaring pigments of modern reds and 'day-glo' effects. Spend a few moments during the day observing, and trying to remember, the different shades of red you see about you. Observe where, and how, red is used, and observe how you are affected by its use. If you own any red clothes, how do you feel when you put them on? How are you affected by other people wearing red clothes?

2. At home, in your meditation space, close your eyes and try to bring some of these reds into your mind's eye. Try to make a visual distinction between pinkish red and deep crimson, or between russet and scarlet. If it helps you to visualise the colour more clearly, bring to mind a particular object you have seen such as a red car, or a neighbour's red front door.

3. In meditation, visualise a scarlet flag, unfurled against the sky on a bright windy day. Visualise the colour of the red flag as pure and vibrant a red as you can imagine. Take as much time as you need to build this image strongly and clearly. See how the flag ripples and unfurls in the wind. Notice how its colour changes as it moves in the wind, the folds creating areas of shade and light that are

constantly shifting. Visualising a moving, changing object is more difficult than visualising a motionless one, but do the best you can for a few minutes and finish your meditation before you become too tired. You are exercising your Inner muscles and they take as much effort to develop as your physical muscles.

4. Your next step is to visualise the flag to be made of the finest silk, and to increase its size so that it fills your vision. Imagine that the sun is behind the flag and shining through the red silk as it billows out against the backdrop of the sky. Notice the effect of the sunlight as it shines through the silk, and see how the colour changes and glows with vibrancy when it is lit by the sun.

5. When you are able to do this easily, imagine that the material substance of the silk flag has disappeared, leaving only the colour. Enjoy watching how the red colour moves and changes in the light, becoming fluid and light-filled. Play with experimenting on how 'thin' or 'thick' you can make the red become so that the sunlight shines more, or less, through it. Watch how it changes. You might find that the flowing colour begins to take on a life of its own, dancing before your eyes, creating moving, fluid shapes. Let it dance, and dance with it. Be joyful in the light and life that is manifesting before you. You are now seeing Faery red!

6. You might like to try this exercise with some of the different shades of red that you have observed and remembered. Notice the different effect of each colour. You may even begin to find that each different shade of red begins to take on its own individual character as if it has become a flowing form that has been adopted by a Faery.

7. Finally, when you are out walking in natural surroundings, allow your vision to soften and let your gaze rest gently on the middle distance. Hold the thought in your mind that you are now able to catch sight of a red Faery hat, or shoes, or jacket, and ask the Faeries to reveal themselves to you in this way.

8. Keep a record of your work, making notes of all that you have achieved and what you found more challenging. Observe how your awareness of the colour red and your sensitivity to its particular vibration increases with practice.

WORKING WITH FAERY ORANGE

An important distinction needs to be made when working with Faeries such as Gwenevere, who is one of the wise and ancient race of immortal 'High Faeries' whose mode of being lies parallel to our own, and the elemental Faeries whose lives are closely linked with the natural world about us. The elemental Faeries, for example, will often take on the characteristics of brightly coloured flowers such that they are almost indivisible from them. These elemental Faeries are an integral part of the green world about us, and although they are unlikely to offer you any great words of wisdom it is comparatively easy, and very enjoyable, to tune in to their presence.

Many of the elemental Faeries whose life-force is coupled with the plant life of the earth are especially fond of the fiery, restless colour orange. Orange is a lively colour on the outer planes but even more so on the Inner planes, and your practical work for this colour should ideally be undertaken out of doors on a hot sunny day.

1. First, as with the colour red, spend some time in tuning your awareness to the colour orange as you see it in your daily environment. The most obvious example of orange is of course an orange fruit, but you will find that the colour in its purest form is not found very frequently. Orange is a vibrant but unsteady colour and is not easy to use.

2. If you can, find some orange flowers, ideally in a quiet garden where you will be undisturbed. Study them closely, observe every shade and tint of their colour, and every delicate detail of their form and shape until you have fixed the image of the flower in your mind.

3. At home, in your meditation space, close your eyes and enter into a meditative and receptive state of mind. Bring the image of the orange flower into your vision, and hold it there until you can see every part of the flower and every different shade and nuance of its colour as clearly as if with your outer sight.

4. When you can do this to your satisfaction, soften your vision until the outlines of the flower dissolve, leaving only the orange colour. Notice how vibrant and alive the colour is. Orange is never static, and you will soon begin to see how it moves and changes, shifting in tone and nuance almost as if it was alive.

5. After you have practised this for a while, you may begin to perceive that the flickering, moving, changing colours in the orange flower

are the dancing presences of the Faeries whose lives are associated with the orange flower you have chosen. Or you may find that the very colour itself begins to speak to you as if it was the fluid form of an Inner presence.

6. After each step, record your results and realisations.

WORKING WITH FAERY YELLOW

As you progress to the colour yellow you will be moving away from the lower end of the visible spectrum and towards the range of vibration which is closer to the world inhabited by the Faeries.

If you were asked to give an example of something yellow, the chances are that you might say 'the sun' just as every child's drawing of the world around her includes a bright yellow sun in a blue sky. In addition to being our source of light and heat, the sun is also a major source of the mysterious all-pervading energy often referred to as Prana, and it is this energy that you will be working with in the following exercises. It is possible to see the sun's Prana under certain circumstances, and to develop the ability to do so will represent a step forward in your ability to perceive the Inner colours and life energies which sustain the Faeries.

There are several well-established techniques of Pranic breathing used in connection with eastern philosophies and spiritual practices, but the following exercises are based on the techniques of the western tradition and are different in their aim and approach. Developing the ability to perceive the colour and energy of Prana will inevitably have a beneficial effect upon you, but these exercises are designed primarily to help you develop your perception of Inner colour and are not intended to be practiced with any means of breath control. When you undertake them, don't focus on your breathing; forget about it, and allow it to take its natural rhythm.

1. As before, observe the different shades of yellow in the world around you. By now you will be more observant of the use of colour in the physical world and more aware of how it affects you. In addition to observing the colour yellow, observe the many different shades of *light* you experience each day. Notice how the morning light differs

from the light at noon, and at sunset. Indoors, observe the different types of artificial light and notice how they affect you. Experience the difference between candle-light, the light of a daylight effect electric light bulb and the harsh glare of fluorescent tubes.

2. Choose a bright, sunny day when the atmosphere is clear and not clouded by haze or pollution. *Carefully avoiding the sun,* look directly up into the blue sky above your head. You will prevent strain on your neck and spine if you do this lying down, or leaning your head against a tree. Soften your gaze, and after a while you will begin to see that the atmosphere is filled with a multitude of tiny twinkling points of diamond light which come and go in an instant. These tiny, fleeting motes of light are the visible manifestation of Prana, the life-force of the sunlight. Realise that this manifestation of life-sustaining energy is all around you. This is the energy that supports the life of the Faeries.

3. Sitting or lying in the sunlight, soften your whole being, and allow the boundaries of your physical body to dissolve. Become aware of the place where you 'end' and the atmosphere about you 'begins' and let the distinction between 'you' and 'not you' begin to fade. Visualise the Prana of Sunlight gently flowing through you, until you have become one with the light.

4. When you have successfully observed and experienced the Prana of the Sunlight out of doors, practice bringing the experience to mind when you sit in meditation indoors, recreating it in your imagination. You will find the experience enlivening, but remember that the chief purpose of the exercise is for you to observe the appearance of Prana with your Inner sight. In your mind's eye, look all around you. Can you observe different qualities of the Prana? Can you see any patterns of movement, or changes in density or brightness? Don't force yourself to see anything, simply remain relaxed and receptive, with a quiet and open mind. Relax the area around your eyes, and soften your Inner vision.

5. When you have gained confidence in observing the visual properties of the energy of Prana, the next stage is to notice how your *consciousness* changes when you open your awareness to its existence.

6. After each session, close down your visualisation, and record your results and realisations. Allow time for further thoughts and ideas to come to you as you write.

WORKING WITH FAERY GREEN

After touching the high levels of the Inner Sunlight of Prana you are now well prepared to step into Green World of Faery. Green is the colour of the heart chakra, and the heart is the real gateway into the Faery kingdom.

1. Observe the many different greens in the world about you, especially when you are walking through woods or natural scenery. This is a good time for you to resume your practice of looking through the corner of your eye. Remember to soften your focus. Don't look directly at anything but allow your gaze to rest gently on the mid-distance. You are not looking at the outward form of things but contacting the Inner light and form which lies just behind the physical.

2. At home, seated in your meditation space, place your attention on your heart chakra. Become mindful of the soft emerald green light of this chakra. Allow this light to expand, until you are sitting within an emerald green sphere of light. Now imagine that the Sun is shining through this sphere of light. Watch how it changes in nuance and intensity as the Prana of Sunlight shines through it. By raising your consciousness and sensitivity to light and colour on the Inner planes, and by visualizing the colours in your imagination, you have created about you a perfect environment for the Faeries. The Faeries will recognise that you have created a sphere of light which matches the level of vibration of their own world. You may become aware that the moving, changing, light-infused Green World you have created about you is becoming infused with the presence of Faery beings who are drawn to you. You are now able to create a gateway into Faery whenever you wish!

3. You might also like to try the same exercise out of doors, in natural surroundings.

4. As always, record your experiences.

VISUALISING GWENEVERE

In addition to developing your sensitivity to light and colour and thus raising your consciousness to the level of the Faeries' world, there is also another, quite different way to approach them. This involves the use of your imagination to deliberately build forms on the Inner planes which the Faeries can adopt in order to come nearer to you, rather as if they were deliberately putting on a set of clothes that you have provided for them. When you use this method you will enable the Faeries to bring down their level of vibration in order to come closer to you on the physical plane, at the same time as you are raising your level of consciousness in order to meet them in their world. You may already have experienced this starting to happen when you deliberately visualized pure colours on the Inner planes. The two methods work hand in hand, and the ideal is to combine them.

It is often thought that the only way to communicate with beings who exist on the Inner planes of creation is to develop the ability to see them objectively, as they really are. But the fact is that those beings who exist on the Inner planes don't have a single, permanent, universally recognisable form. Their form is fluid and transient, and the further they are from the level of our physical world the more subtle and changeable their form will be. The Faeries' plane of existence is comparatively close to our own, so their form retains some degree of permanence, but if you have ever wondered why you come across so many different and often contradictory descriptions of Faeries, the reason is that everyone does indeed see them differently. Everyone's description of the Faeries they have seen will be true in the sense that each description accurately conveys each person's individual perception at that time. But because all Inner plane beings flow from one form to another, and because each person's description of them will be coloured by their own personal perception, there will be some variation in what they perceive.

A question often asked is whether you have really seen a Faery on the Inner planes or whether you have just imagined the Faery to be there, as if these two concepts of 'real' and 'imagined' were mutually exclusive. When you are working on the Inner levels of creation the two concepts are very similar. The images and forms you create with your imagination provide the form for the Faeries to inhabit, if they wish. By actively using your imagination, you are building forms upon the Inner planes where communication between the worlds can take place.

When you are working with Gwenevere in the following chapters, you can use the power of your imagination to create a form for her to adopt. When you do this successfully you will be in no doubt of when she enters into the form you have built for her. Contacting Gwenevere in this way does not mean that you have invented her, or that you are just imagining her in the sense that you are fantasizing, or that she is not really there. When she appears to you in a form you have built for her, she is no less real. She is simply using the Inner form you have provided, stepping down her level of vibration in order to be nearer to you. So the more definition and clarity you can give to your image the better, and you will see why it is also very important that you create a *suitable* image.

As part of the process of creating a suitable magical image for Gwenevere, it's best to rid yourself of any preconceptions you may have of her appearance, in order that you can start with a clean slate. So, jot down any words of description which come to mind you when you think of her...

You may not have found this easy. Part of the problem is that a record of Gwenevere has barely survived through the channels of myth and legend. The picture of King Arthur on horseback, handsomely kitted out in a suit of shining armour and brandishing a magnificent sword, is a strong one in popular imagination even though it probably does not bear any relation to his original appearance. But it has become embedded in our culture and serves as an Inner plane image which the real King Arthur can inhabit. When you thought of Queen Gwenevere you might perhaps have been tempted to clothe her in the embroidered robes and tall pointed hat of a mediaeval lady? But because Gwenevere is a Faery, not a mediaeval lady, images like this are not entirely appropriate and can even act as a barrier between you. So let us now build a suitable image for Gwenevere to clothe herself in.

The description which follows has been carefully built up over a period of time, and because it has already acquired some solidity of form on the Inner planes it will be comparatively easy for you to tune in to. If you are working on your own, read the description several times until you can remember it, then close your eyes in meditation and start to build the form with your imagination. Visualise each separate part of her appearance with as much intention, clarity and detail as you are able. If you are working with a partner or in a group, you can take it in turns to read the description aloud to each other. If you are reading the description to others, read it slowly, and with a pause between each phrase, as this will give your companions sufficient time to build the image in their mind's eye.

Enter your meditation space, light a candle, relax and soften your mind and, with quiet respect for the Faery being you are about to call towards you, slowly and carefully begin to build her image. When you have built the image to your satisfaction, softly speak Gwenevere's name. It is your genuine intention and desire to make contact with her rather than the volume of your voice that is likely to attract her attention.

Gwenevere is a little taller than most humans. Like many Faeries, her appearance is similar to that of humans, but her form is more fluid and less solid. Her body seems to be infused with light so her overall appearance is of white, shining light, as if infused with Prana. She wears flowing robes, but they are made of a substance which is not woven from any recognisable earthly material. The finest spun silk is perhaps the nearest equivalent.

Her robes are predominately a most beautiful shining silvery-white, with faint shadows of blue-violet, and palest green. They seem to hold light, while also allowing light to shine through them. You find that as she moves, the colour of her robes appears to change according to her surroundings, and also according to an Inner light which shines through her.

Visualise Gwenevere standing amongst trees. You will see that her robes pick up and reflect the green of the leaves.

Now visualise Gwenevere standing among brightly coloured flowers, and see how their colour is also picked up by her robes. There is a constant movement of light around and within her.

Become aware of a glimpse of Gwenevere's shoes underneath her robe. They are pale emerald green. Now visualise her standing upon a sward of green grass which is covered with tiny white flowers like daisies, and which are a mirror-image of the star-filled sky.

Look carefully at the colour of her skin. Like her robes, it changes according to her surroundings, and you will be able to see the flowing energy beneath the surface.

She has long hair of the palest gold, but the substance of her hair is not as human hair and if you try to touch it with your fingers you will find that it dissolves beneath your touch into something less than tangible. See how her hair is filled with golden motes of light, like star-dust.

She wears a tall crown. The shape of her crown is not like any earthly crown, and its appearance changes, sometimes seeming very tall, and at other times appearing more like a simple band or diadem. It is not made of earthly metals or jewels, although it has something of both these substances within it. It is formed of strands of gold filigree which have been spun so thin that almost nothing of their material substance remains.

The jewels in her crown are not solid, but reveal the fluid essence of precious gemstones, as if their wonderful colours were somehow distilled into liquid starlight. These colours are not fixed, but slowly change according to the nature of the energy which surrounds her. Her crown is not for decorative or ceremonial purposes but is an outward expression of her own consciousness, rather like the crown chakra of humans, and its appearance changes just as the crown chakra will reflect the condition of human spiritual awareness.

Her crown forms her connection with the stars. The stellar fires, with all their jewelled colours, are as much a part of her consciousness and life-energy as is the Sun in our human consciousness.

Now visualise Gwenevere standing underneath a star-lit sky. Her pale golden hair, filled with star-dust, is moved gently by the winds of space.

When you have built her appearance in your mind's eye, wait until you feel that she is aware of you and has made contact with you. You may perhaps be aware of this simply as an indefinable exchange of energy rather than anything more tangible. This may happen straight away, or you may need to return to the meditation on later occasions.

When you have finished your meditation session, clearly and deliberately make this evident to Gwenevere, and visualise her turning away from you and fading from your sight. Don't keep her hanging around. She needs to know when you are concluding your communication with her, just as would be the case in any human conversation.

You will find, perhaps straight away, or perhaps with more persistence, that something happens during this meditation. You may find it hard to put into words what has happened, but something will feel different about the image you have built, and you yourself will feel different as a result. You will know when Gwenevere has entered the image you have built for her.

After you have made contact with Gwenevere, continue to build her image regularly in meditation, and with an open mind. Don't rush, don't force anything, and don't hold any pre-conceptions as to what might happen, particularly as to anything you might *want* to happen. You are trying to establish a channel of communication, so you must keep an open mind and be receptive to what Gwenevere might want to communicate to you. Remember that she also needs to be able to get to know you and find out who you are.

After a while, you may find that you can hear what she is saying to you, or that you know that she is communicating something to you even though she doesn't use words. You may find that ideas or concepts appear in your head which you can unravel later when the meditation session has finished. Her voice may sound like pure song, or the music of the wind in the trees, or you may hear her voice as a human voice.

In this and all the following exercises, keep in mind that although Faeries are different to humans, they are neither superior nor inferior to humanity. Faeries are not Gods and Goddesses, and it is inappropriate to offer them devotion. Their appearance is often one of great beauty, but do not allow yourself to become glamorised by them. Faeries have much to teach us, but it is equally true to say that we have much to offer them in return. Be aware that Gwenevere may well have questions to ask you!

You may also find that when you have successfully made contact with Gwenevere she will begin to introduce you to others of her Faery world. Trust your own instincts, and if you feel unsure of anyone who appears to you, you can politely and firmly end the contact. It can often facilitate the process of communication if you come to the meditation session with a question, as this will help to focus your attention. You might also like to ask her to introduce you to some of the members of her family, but again, be prepared for surprises and do not allow your preconceptions to cloud what she shows to you.

In all your communications with the Faeries, never try to coerce, and never allow yourself to be coerced. If at any time you feel uneasy, simply open your eyes, extinguish your candle, and have a cup of tea. Do not expect the Faeries to have the same approach to life as you. Their concept of right and wrong is not the same as ours, and just as your approach to the Faery race should always be one of honour and respect, so also you should expect the same from them in return.

Here are two examples of how you might like to communicate with Gwenevere.

GWENEVERE AND THE SACRED EARTH

Either indoors or outdoors, contact Gwenevere by building her image, and respectfully invite her towards you. When you have established communication with her, ask her to demonstrate, in whatever way she chooses, how she relates to the Earth. Ask how she perceives the physical world you inhabit. Ask her about the Faeries' relationship with the planet earth. Ask what their relationship is with humanity.

These are profound questions, and will elicit complex answers which may not always be easy to hear. But it is only when you have gained some understanding of the Faeries' attitude towards humankind that you can begin to move forward with them, in a realistic manner, into our shared future.

As a final exercise, you might like to ask Gwenevere if she will permit you to look at the physical world *through her eyes*. This exercise can provide you with some valuable insights, not only into the Faeries' point of view of your own world but also of the universal energies which underpin all living things. If she agrees, you will find it easiest if you ask her to stand behind you and to bring her aura closely into contact with your own. Don't think about this too hard but just do it, believing that it can be done. Try looking at trees through her eyes, or at fire, or water, or any object in the material world.

At first, you will probably find it easier to do this while in a quite deep meditation. But once you have acquired the ability, you will find it a useful technique to adopt from time to time in many different circumstances, both in the Inner and outer worlds. You will use it to good effect in a later chapter. Don't use it too often though, and always make sure to return fully into your own body when you have finished, allowing Gwenevere to completely break the contact with you.

This concludes the preliminary exercises for raising the level of your consciousness to that of the Faery realms, but you can return to them whenever you feel the need to work on improving and increasing your awareness of the Faeries and their world. The contact you have made with Gwenevere will form an essential basis for the more detailed work in the Mysteries of Round Table that follows.

CHAPTER FOUR

The Round Table and the Five Faery Kingdoms

IN CHAPTER TWO, we gathered together the many levels of meaning and symbolism contained in the Round Table. The Round Table itself, and the work of the magical Order associated with it, was guarded in turn by Faeries and humans, having been made by Merlin for Uther PenDragon, then passing to Gwenevere's Faery father Leodegrance, and finally given to King Arthur. After Gwenevere's death it returned to her Faery kindred, although our exploration of this must wait until later chapters.

When Merlin introduced the Round Table into Uther PenDragon's court he was initially responsible for establishing the system of teaching that provided the foundation for this school of Inner wisdom, a system that derived from ancient, perhaps Atlantean magical practices. Once he had achieved this, he retreated from the outer world and was seen only very rarely on the physical plane. Gwenevere then took on the role of Initiator into its Mysteries, especially those aspects connected with Faery, and with the Grail. But how did this magical organisation actually work in practice?

The answer is provided by the Arthurian and Grail legends themselves. The majority of the stories of King Arthur and the knights of the Round Table are a record of how the knights learnt and practiced their magical skills. The definition of magic as 'the art of raising consciousness according to will' can hardly be bettered, and this was the foundation of the knights' work. In addition, most Western Mystery systems share the same ultimate goal: to Know

Yourself, and the Order of the Round Table was no exception to this.

Typically, the path to self knowledge begins when the Seeker or neophyte, realising that they are unhappy or unfulfilled in the circumstances of their life, begin to look at why this might be so and what they can do about it. The journey to self discovery may well start with learning about the habitual patterns of defensive behaviour that can become inbuilt from the earliest childhood experiences and traumas, colouring one's reactions to later experiences and resulting in a tendency to repeat the same mistakes over again. The Seeker learns about the strengths and weaknesses of the personality, and begins to recognise the repressed parts of the psyche that are sometimes called the 'shadow.' When some of these habitual defensive patterns have been cleared, the Seeker is better able to form loving relationships and to function as an integrated and useful member of society. In other words, he or she becomes 'ordinary!'

In esoteric circles or Mystery Schools, this first stage is often referred to as the Outer Court and in the Arthurian stories it is literally so: the knights experience this stage when they become involved in the numerous adventures that take place outside the court of the Round Table and before they have been accepted into its circle. Arthur's kingdom of Logres is a mysterious land that hovers on the border between the outer and Inner worlds. The castles, people and places that appear throughout these stories are tenuously linked with actual locations in the physical landscape but they are empowered by Inner forces that offer the knights a succession of tests and challenges, victories and defeats. This represents the stage of clearing, healing and renewal that appears to take place within Arthur's kingdom but is actually happening within the psyche. This is the first stage in the journey to the Self, a period of searching for the path through dark forests, where the forces of the psyche manifest as strange beasts and where the wounds suffered by the knights are of the mind and emotions rather than the body.

In this strange landscape it is often Merlin who is in command of the raw elemental forces that sometimes threaten to overcome the knights, and we can therefore identify him as the Magus or tutelary spirit behind this stage of the spiritual journey. In the Vulgate Cycle he is often shown in this role, raising a mist, causing a river to flood, blowing a horn to arouse the woods and creating rainstorms and dust clouds. His role is represented by the dragon he carries as a banner.

The dragon appears at times to be made of brass, but is magically light in weight and capable of turning the air red with flame. The red dragon represents the driving energy of the human body that is sometimes referred to as the Kundalini, and the dragon's transformation from brass to pure flame symbolises how the human will can become transformed into the pure energy of fire through its proper alignment with God's Will.

With Merlin's help, King Arthur brings his kingdom into a state of balance and harmony in which his enemies are defeated or brought under control, a process that is then repeated by his knights. This stage symbolises the deep healing within the psyche of the Seeker and is an essential stage in the path to self knowledge. In ancient civilisations this process was all part of the work of a Mystery School although nowadays it is generally achieved in the separate disciplines of counselling and psychotherapy. Many Seekers find that when their early wounds have been healed, the very same qualities that were initially so challenging later become transformed into their own unique and special strength.

The next stage on the path to self discovery is when the Seeker, who is now reasonably secure in his or her self, begins to explore the Inner worlds, often initially by acquiring knowledge of one of the many 'maps' of the Inner worlds which provide a working template of the principles that operate throughout the universe. The Seeker may well then join a group in which this knowledge is put into practice. Such a group will typically espouse a strong relationship with Deity, will offer a developed and coherent teaching of the universal patterns that permeate the whole of creation from the starry constellations to the smallest particle, will promote an understanding of the laws and cycles of life, death and rebirth, and will have a well established practice of communication with certain wise teachers who guide the group from the Inner planes of creation.

This is exactly what the Order of the Round Table provides, and the Vulgate Cycle describes the different orders or 'esoteric grades' that existed within the Order as a whole. The Knights of the Round Table continued to be the foremost of these, but there was also a group known as the Queen's Knights which was led by Gawain. The purpose of this group was to offer personal support to any knight who sought assistance in fighting with another knight, man to man, wherever this fight took place. One of the features of this particular Order was that each knight promised to give a full report of his adventures to the others so that they could learn from them – a habit which to this day remains an important discipline within many esoteric groups.

Another group was called the Knights of the Watch, which we may assume was in charge of the maintenance and protection of the court from threats to its safety deriving from both the outer and Inner worlds. A third group was known as the Table of Errant Companions, and the work of this group would have been devoted to seeking challenge and adventure further afield, finding ways in which to extend the boundaries of knowledge and ability within the Order. This work would of course have taken place on the Inner planes, not within the outer world. Last – and perhaps least – was the Table of Less-Valued Knights whose purpose we can only surmise!

But the particular and special emphasis to the Mysteries of the Round Table was the specific purpose of teaching its students about the Faery race and their world, and working towards healing the rift between Faery and human that occurred early in our shared history and which is intimately associated with the health of the planet we share. And beyond even this especial focus on the two races of Faery and human, is the additional level of meaning to be found in the Mysteries of the Round Table that addresses the internal, subjectively experienced division between the Faery and human elements that can be experienced within the individual's own psyche. We might perhaps refer to this as 'the Faery within.' The ultimate goal of all these Mysteries of the Round Table, and which is intimately linked with the meaning of the Grail, is to find the way to discover and heal this dichotomy so that we can then move on towards a reintegration of the one, same, shared root and source of our being, Faery and human together. This works both objectively and subjectively, within and without.

Although Merlin was initially responsible for establishing these Mysteries, he did not teach them within the court of the Round Table. He made an occasional appearance when things went wrong and reached a crisis, but in the Arthurian legends the role of teacher is almost entirely taken by women. It is the Faery women who typically make the initial contact with the knights and encourage and cajole them to face the next challenge in their Inner journey. The Lady of the Lake oversees their work from the Inner planes and, like Merlin, makes an occasional direct intervention into the mundane world at times of crisis. But it is Gwenevere who is immediately, and consistently, responsible for initiating the opportunities, challenges and lessons of the Mysteries of the Round Table.

She did so primarily by forging a connection between the court of the Round Table and the five Faery Kingdoms which lie close to its borders. As we mentioned in Chapter One, these kingdoms are Lyonesse (sometimes called Carmelide), Sorelois, Gorre, Oriande and Listenois. These five kingdoms correspond closely with the basic magical and universal pattern commonly found in the Western Mystery Tradition, that of a quartered circle around a central point. This is often also represented as an equal-armed cross upon whose centre blooms a perfect rose.

In this magical system, each of the four quarters represents an aspect of the Sun's journey through the sky in relation to the earth in its daily and yearly cycle. Each quarter is associated with one of the four cardinal directions and is also linked with a variety of spiritual, psychological and physical attributes that correspond with the Sun's daily and yearly cycles.

For example, as the Sun rises in the East, the Eastern quarter of the magical circle is traditionally associated with qualities that correspond with the idea of dawn, such as physical or spiritual rebirth, renewal and healing, the dawning light of inspiration, new ideas and concepts, and above all the concept of spiritual direction, of finding one's own true destiny and purpose.

Moving clockwise around the circle to the South we arrive at the point where the Sun reaches its zenith at noon, and where its full power symbolises the strength and command that we may achieve over ourselves and demonstrate in the accomplishments of our outer lives. It represents the height of our attainment in the outer world, and acknowledges the courage and determination that we have used in order to reach that position.

In the West, the Sun's imminent descent below the horizon represents the change that occurs within our own psyche when our focus in life shifts from the demands of the mundane world to our relationship with the more subtle energies of the Inner worlds. Just as the Sun appears to lessen in accessible heat and strength as it descends in the sky so too do we have less energy for the demands of the outer world and needs must find the resources that lie within us. This change in our consciousness can lead to an increased awareness of the Inner worlds, and for some, it marks the period when the journey inwards eventually leads to an experience of Initiation in which the Inner life becomes increasingly and substantially more real.

Finally, the Northern quarter of the magical circle represents the hidden sun at midnight. With no visible sunlight to illumine the way, the Seeker must rely solely on his or her own inner light and resources built up from past experience and lessons learned. The night sky is lit only by the stars, so this quarter also represents the concept of a symbolic death to the physical world that opens the gateway to the secrets of the hidden wisdom. This quarter simultaneously symbolises the revelations of the starry sky and the deep wisdom of the Inner earth, and can lead to the realisation that the two are intimately related.

Because the symbolism and mysteries of the Round Table are thoroughly rooted in the Western Magical tradition, four of the Faery Kingdoms fit precisely into these quarters and exemplify the same traditional set of correspondences. And, just as the centre of the circle customarily represents their culmination on a higher level and brings through the divine light of spirit which shines on the whole circle, so at the centre of the four Faery Kingdoms we find Listenois, the Kingdom of the Grail. This pattern is shown below.

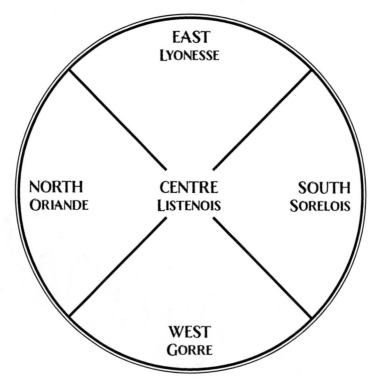

In the following chapters each of these kingdoms will be explored in much greater detail, but a brief description here will show how this basic plan falls into place. Lyonesse is placed in the East because it is the kingdom of Gwenevere's birth and childhood, and the stories which describe her birth and early years shed considerable light on her later role in the court of the Round Table. In addition, we will also find that her father Leodegrance is a significant figure in the interpretation of the symbolism of the Round Table. As we noted in Chapter Two, it was with good reason that Merlin entrusted the guardianship of the Round Table to Leodegrance, who continues to function as guide and interpreter of its wisdom, providing a real and lasting source of inspiration alongside his daughter Gwenevere.

Sorelois is placed in the South, because this kingdom represents the idea of rulership and Sovereignty: it explores the concept of our King-or-Queenship over our own selves, within our environment and especially in our relationship with the Faery realms. Gwenevere spent a period of three years in the Kingdom of Sorelois while she was married to King Arthur, and during this period she was crowned as its Queen. Sorelois offers us the opportunity to understand the challenges posed by the concept of rulership, authority and command, particularly in our relationship with Faery.

Gorre is placed in the West because it deals with the challenges that arise when we begin to turn towards the Inner life, and take the initiatory journey into the deeper levels of Faery. Gwenevere travelled into Gorre and spent some time there while she was married to King Arthur. The path she took was later followed by Lancelot of the Lake, and the story of Lancelot's eventful and initiatory passage into Gorre is as important as the qualities of the Kingdom itself. By following Gwenevere into Gorre, Lancelot opens up the way for others to follow him. The challenges of this journey are not of physical ability or authority within the outer world but of purpose and belief: we are tested in our motives for wanting to journey into Faery and we can experience, with Lancelot, the doubts and fears that must be overcome if we are to progress.

Oriande is placed in the North, because it represents the Mysteries of the Inner earth and the stars within the earth, and forms a gateway into a different level of the wisdom of the Round Table. This little known Faery kingdom is the home of Gwenevere's Faery kindred. Her Faery family makes a late appearance in the legends, and its primary concern is the fate of the Round Table after Gwenevere's death. Oriande provides us with the opportunity to look at the world and its human inhabitants through Faery eyes, and to understand the Mysteries of the Round Table from the Faeries' point of view. It is in the Kingdom of Oriande that the stellar mysteries embedded with the Round Table are revealed, and the journey into this kingdom takes us into the higher levels of its magical symbolism.

Finally, the fifth and central Faery Kingdom is Listenois, wherein is found the Castle of the Grail and the company of beings, Faery and human, who guard it. Here, the Innermost mysteries of the Round Table are revealed, but they can only be fully understood by those who have successfully undergone the challenges represented by the other four Faery Kingdoms.

The four quarters of the magical circle are summed up by the traditional adage of the magician: To Know, to Dare, to Will and to Keep Silent, and we find that these are also represented by the Faery kingdoms. Lyonesse symbolises the ability to Know. Sorelois symbolises the ability to Dare. In Gorre you will work with the attributes of the Will which are associated with the quality of Spiritual Desire. In Oriande you will discover the deep silence of the starry skies. This four-fold division of the circle is an expression of the Rose Cross that forms the basis of the Atlantean Mysteries of the West. The perfect rose which blooms at the centre when the four quarters are brought into balance and fullness of expression is represented by the Grail Kingdom of Listenois.

The following chapters will take you on a series of magical journeys into each of these Faery Kingdoms in turn, so that you can experience their gifts and challenges for yourself. You will be guided in each journey by Gwenevere.

As a means of grounding your magical work, it is suggested that you design and make your own symbolic Round Table! It will become your own magical talisman, linked in your mind and imagination to the infinite wisdom contained within the Round Table of the Inner worlds, and it will continue to act as a magical symbol of all that you learn and experience while undertaking this work. As a start, keep the above diagram of the quartered circle in mind, learn the names of the Faery Kingdoms and their position in the circle, and begin to think of possible symbols that you might use to represent them.

Your model can be worked on as you progress through the book, and can be as grand or simple as your imagination and budget permit.

For example, it could be a coloured drawing on a piece of paper, a painted mandala on a floor-cloth or perhaps an arrangement of symbolic objects that can be taken out, moved around, and tidied away as necessary. You might like to use crystals, or coloured candles, or you can make a series of drawings that represent your current understanding of the table's symbolism. Whatever shape or form it takes, your model will provide a focus for your thoughts and realisations, it will help you to ground your work into the earth plane, and it will acquire real talismanic significance because of the Inner connections you have made. Most importantly, it will not be a reproduction of any preconceived ideas you may have of what the Round Table should look like, or of artists' images of it that you have seen in illustrated books of the Arthurian legends, but will be an expression of your own individual interpretation of its meaning.

One of the most important symbols in any work with Faery is that of the mirror, and indeed it could be said that the Round Table you construct as your magical talisman will function as a mirror between the worlds. When you begin to approach the world of Faery you may well begin to experience a number of strange signs or coincidences cropping up in your life that are connected with the concept of 'mirroring' or 'twinning', for example the experience of a series of events where things seem to be happening in pairs. Sometimes this phenomenon can be associated with a sense of *deja-vu* that leaves you with the feeling that you have experienced it before. Or you may begin to get a sense that you are seeing things from a different point of view, as if what you have habitually perceived as reality is really a mirror image and that you are now viewing it as if from the other side of the glass.

You may also find during your work with Faeries that the concept of a sister or brother keeps cropping up in your life, perhaps giving you the impression that someone who feels *as if* they were your brother or sister, is coming closer to you. In meditation work you may meet a Faery being who feels like a lost part of yourself, as if you have discovered a part of yourself that you didn't realise was there. Faeries often make and retain contact with a particular human family through many generations, a process which can continue for hundreds of years even though some of those generations may not be aware of them. Faery companions were readily acknowledged by our early ancestors but a lack of written records together with a more recent reluctance to talk about these things means that for the most part we are not aware of the Faeries who may have accompanied our family through the centuries. When we rediscover them, believing that we have contacted them for the first time, this can often be accompanied by an unexplained impression of familiarity. And there is also a more fundamental bonding which occurs between a human and a Faery through many lifetimes, as if they were once a single entity.

The symbol of a mirror functions in the same way as any traditional symbolic gateway between the Inner and outer worlds such as a veil hung between two pillars. But rather than functioning simply as a veil or barrier which can be passed through, the mirror also represents the fact that the human and Faery worlds exist in a reflective relationship with each other, a relationship in which they are linked at many levels, just as humans and Faeries are linked at many levels. This mirroring phenomenon is not a general characteristic of the Inner planes of creation but is especially found in the relationship between Faery and human and you will probably find that the further you walk into the Faery world, the stronger and more intense this mirroring effect becomes.

The reason for this stems from the unique relationship between us; we are of the same root. In cosmic terms we are one and the same, and in the very earliest days of our existence we were one. The further we walk into the Faery mirror, the nearer we approach our common source of origin. Thus our journey into Faery is one of healing and balance, of reconciliation and remembering, not only between the two separated races but of the elements of both that are within our psyche. Every time you pass through the mirror into Faery, any action you take, or lessons you learn, or experiences of the Faery world you make real in your daily life, will equally affect both Faery and human worlds. The greatest paradox of this work is the closer you become to Faery, the nearer you become to your Self.

The remainder of this chapter is a guided Inner journey in which you will be led to the chamber of the Round Table that lies at the heart of these Mysteries. This journey is one you will take many times in the following chapters, and from now on all your journeys into the Faery Kingdoms will begin from this chamber. You will find your own seat waiting for you at the Round Table, and you will always be joined by Gwenevere, who will be your mentor throughout each journey. You may also find that you are joined by others at the Round Table, Faery and human. As with all Inner work, the more often you build this scene in your imagination the more real it will become, and after a while it will begin to act as a beacon to those who work on the Inner planes and who will be drawn to working with you.

As with the guided meditation that led you to Gwenevere in Chapter Three, this journey can be taken on your own, or with a partner or a group. If you are working on your own, read it through several times beforehand so that you have it firmly in your mind and can then take yourself through it without having to open your eyes to read it. If you are working with a partner or group you can take it in turns to read it aloud. If you are reading it aloud to others, the key to doing this successfully is to speak much more slowly than your normal rate of speech, and to leave a brief pause after every phrase. This may feel odd at first, but it will allow plenty of time for the others to build each image in their imagination. If you read too quickly it will simply become a story to listen to rather than a journey into the Inner planes.

JOURNEY TO THE CHAMBER OF THE ROUND TABLE

If you have already begun to make your talismanic Round Table, place it before you in your meditation space.

Begin your journey by lighting a candle, and saying:

"I light this candle in recognition of the One Deity who made heaven and earth, the stars and the planets, animals and minerals, Faery and human, and all who share in creation. May we live in peace and harmony, together in the Light."

You have travelled a long way, and your journey has taken you through a great forest. The way through the trees has not always been easy to discover, and several paths you took with confidence seemed to lead nowhere, or led you into a tangle of undergrowth. But you have successfully come through these challenges and the dark forest now lies behind you.

Before you lies a wide lake. Its waters are calm and unruffled by any wind. A white mist hovers over its surface, and you cannot see its far side. You are standing on a narrow beach of white sand that rims the shore. A small boat rests at the edge of lake, nearby. You walk over to it, step into it, and take your seat. The boat glides into the water and away from the shore. It heads slowly across the lake into the mist.

As you move silently across the waters, the white mist thickens, and soon you lose sight of the shore. But you continue to make headway, and after a while you can see the shape of an island looming ahead of you out of the mist, in the centre of the lake. As you get nearer, it begins to shine out more clearly, and you can see the outline of what seems to be a castle, with tall, white towers. Sometimes you can see only a single watchtower, sometimes you can see several towers. The castle seems to change under your gaze, as if it was constantly transforming in response to an invisible force.

The boat reaches the shore of the island. You step out onto white sand. But although the mist has now cleared, the shining, ethereal castle has completely disappeared, as if it was only an illusion. All that lies before you now is a grassy mound, of some considerable size, covered in tiny white flowers.

There is an opening in the side of the mound, just about your own height. It is marked by crystalline stones on either side, and upon the lintel. You walk forward and stand for a moment in the space between the crystalline stones. You experience a strange change of atmosphere, as if the air was becoming almost electric. And as you stand there, your eyes begin to adjust to the darkness of the space inside the mound, and you can see inside.

You realise that the chamber within the mound is much larger than you would have imagined. In fact the longer you stand there, the larger it becomes. Having realised this strange reality, you wait until the chamber has grown to a great size.

You step inside, and look about you. The chamber is circular, with a high domed roof. At the centre of the chamber is a large Round Table. There are many figures seated about the table in quiet meditation. Your attention is drawn to the seated figure of Gwenevere. She looks up, and becomes aware of your presence. You make your contact with her, a little relieved to see a familiar figure. She seems to expect you to say something, so you take a moment to find the words which will express your reason for coming here...

When you have found the right words (you may wish to prepare them beforehand) speak them slowly, either out loud, or silently and deliberately. You may also like to identify yourself by speaking your name.

And now, you realise that there is a seat at the Round Table waiting for you. It has your name on it, although perhaps it is a private name that you reserve for magical work. You take your place, and join the company of those who serve in these Mysteries. You look about you, and perhaps recognise some of those who are seated there. Take as much time as you need to make your contact with those who are seated here.

The table itself is made of a dark crystalline substance. At its centre there is a golden bowl, in which burns a perpetual flame. A faint perfume of roses emanates from within the bowl. The bowl, and the flame, and the faint perfume, impart an air of inviolability to the chamber.

As you look across the surface of the table, you realise that it is like a great mirror to the night skies, and you can see the shapes of the starry constellations within its depths.

The chamber is oriented to the four cardinal directions. A veil hangs at each of the four quarters. You realise that this chamber stands at the centre of the five Faery Kingdoms. Each veil forms a gateway.

In the **East**, a pale blue veil hangs before the gateway into Lyonesse.
In the **South**, a pale golden veil hangs before the gateway into Sorelois.
In the **West**, a violet veil hangs before the gateway into Gorre.
In the **North**, a silver veil hangs before the gateway into Oriande.

At the centre of the table, the golden bowl and perpetual flame represent the gateway into Listenois.

Later, you will pass through each of these gateways in turn, and journey into each of these Faery Kingdoms. But for now, it is sufficient that you observe all that lies about you, and take sufficient time to build the scene clearly in your imagination.

You take the opportunity to renew your contact with Gwenevere. Be receptive to anything she may wish to communicate to you.

When you are ready, make a respectful gesture of thanks to those who have gathered in the chamber of the Round Table with you, and make your way out through the doorway in the side of the mound. The boat is waiting for you. You climb in, and it takes you back across the water. When you have stepped out onto the shore, you turn to find that the lake, and the island, have disappeared. You have returned to your own place and time.

CHAPTER FIVE

The Faery Kingdom of Sorelois

NOW THAT YOU HAVE FOUND your way to the Innerworld chamber of the Round Table and taken your place amongst those who continue to work within these Mysteries, you are ready to be guided by Gwenevere into the five Faery Kingdoms. The first of these is the Kingdom of Sorelois. The stories of each of these kingdoms will be described to you in turn, in the following chapters, so you don't need to have any previous familiarity with them. The original complete stories are fascinating and can be very rewarding to read, but they are quite long, and are often padded out with an endless succession of battles! If you would like to read them in full, you will find references to them at the end of each chapter.[1]

All these journeys will be undertaken in your imagination in just the same way as you travelled to the chamber of the Round Table. Each journey begins and ends at the Round Table, where you can meet and make contact with Gwenevere, benefit from her guidance, and share what you have learnt with the other companions of the Order of the Round Table who join you there. Each journey requires you to explore a different aspect of your relationship with the Faeries and their world, and will give you plenty of opportunity to meet some of the many Faery beings who play such an important part in the Arthurian legends. In this way, you will join with them in building bridges between human and Faery.

Each of the Faery kingdoms is associated with a group of magical symbols, qualities and attributes which represent the essential meaning of the kingdom. In addition to the suggestions given below, you may well find that additional symbols occur to you as you progress, and you can add these to your talismanic Round Table as you work with each kingdom in turn.

MAGICAL CORRESPONDENCES OF THE KINGDOM OF SORELOIS	
Direction:	South
Symbol:	A golden crown
Challenges:	Fear, pride, glamour
Gifts:	Sovereignty
Initiators:	Gwenevere, Galehaut

THE FAERY KINGDOM OF SORELOIS

Sorelois is ruled by one of the lesser-known figures of Arthurian legend: the Faery Prince Galehaut. His name is similar to the better-known Galahad, one of knights of the Round Table who reached the Grail Castle, but there is no connection between the two characters apart from their similarity of name.

Galehaut is descended from the race of giants that appears frequently in the background to the Arthurian legends, as they do in many world mythologies. But this ancient and mysterious race was regarded with ambivalence even at the time that the Arthurian legends were first recorded, where they are referred to with some uncertainty as to whether they are friend or foe. A proper study has yet to be made of this race, but in the Arthurian legends at least, giants seem more often to be identified as the remote ancestors of Faeries rather than of humans.

In fact Galehaut was descended from two giants. His mother was known simply as the Beautiful Giantess, and his father was a giant named Brunor, who inhabited the Castle of Tears on the Giant's Isle. But just as Rion's kingdom of the Grasslands was shunned because of the strange phenomena that occurred there, so it was said that the customs of the Giant's Isle were such that Galehaut was driven away to seek his own land, and he acquired Sorelois by overcoming its original ruler. Perhaps there is a faint memory here of a separation between the giants and Faeries that occurred in remote times when one race gained prominence over the other.

The actual location of Sorelois is defined with the same inimitable mixture of lucidity and obscurity that is bestowed on most of the named locations in the Arthurian legends. It is described with confidence as being adjacent to Cornwall yet also lying between Wales and the 'Distant Isles,' as being adjacent to Logres but separated from it by a body of salt water (this makes it sound rather like Anglesey), while simultaneously being a neighbour to the Kingdom of the Franks and yet separated from it by the River Humber. In other words it can be found to the Northwest, Southwest, centre and Northeast of England.

Clearly this makes no sense if we try to interpret it as fact, but in terms of the dynamics of the Inner worlds it makes a great deal of sense. Arthur's kingdom of Logres represents the centre of the land of Britain, and in many respects Logres represents the physical plane.[2] Closely linked with Logres, and surrounding it on all quarters, although not manifesting on the physical plane, are the Innerworld kingdoms of Faery. They are usually separated from Logres by a 'river.' Passage across the river is often long, and usually perilous. For example, Sorelois was said to be separated from Logres by two wooden causeways, high and narrow, each eight miles long and in places 400 hundred feet under water! At the head of each causeway was a defensive tower, tall and strong.

Again, this cannot be taken literally, but as an evocation of the Inner space that must be crossed in order to reach these Faery kingdoms it serves very well. 'Water' is an apt metaphor for the etheric levels that closely border the physical world, and the experience of moving through this level into the Inner worlds that lie beyond can often feel like crossing a narrow bridge: it's easy to lose your concentration and fall off! As will be discussed later, the etheric waters which divide Logres from the world of Faery are guarded by the Lady of the Lake who guides, instructs and supervises those who undertake this rite of passage.

Together with Gwenevere, Galehaut plays a prominent role in the challenges presented by this Faery Kingdom, and because he has remained comparatively unknown for so long you may well find when you meet him in your imaginative journeys that he comes through particularly clearly. Galehaut has a unique relationship with Gwenevere. He was not married, and did not have a Queen of his own, but Gwenevere spent three years with him in Sorelois when, for reasons we shall explore later in this chapter, she was exiled from Arthur's kingdom. For these three years, Galehaut ruled in partnership with

Gwenevere who became the Faery Queen of Sorelois. During these three years King Arthur was besotted with another woman, and his kingdom of Logres became waste and barren.

The meaning of this episode is closely linked with the concept of rulership and Sovereignty, a concept that is perfectly expressed by the appearance of one of Galehaut's castles in Sorelois. The favourite of his many castles, it was named 'The Proud Fortress' and stood on solid rock high above a swift-running stream. Galehaut said that he found this castle so uplifting that however downcast he felt when he entered it, he never failed to be restored by its joyful power. The castle consisted simply of an enclosing wall and central tower, and the wall and top of the tower were both deeply crenellated.

In the Faery kingdoms, 'castles' are centres of energy, not actual buildings of bricks and mortar. They indicate places where energy is more defined and 'thicker', and their energetic form can be likened to a vortex or whirlpool. Often, these castles are described as spiralling or turning in a circle for the simple reason that they are doing just that. Each castle has a particular character or focus that is indicated by its name, and together they form a 'map' of the Inner worlds that was an important part of the magical training of the knights of the Round Table. In their exploration of the Inner worlds the knights would spend time in each of these castles, learning what it represented and experiencing its qualities.

Galehaut describes his vision of how this castle might appear in its most perfect and glorious form as a symbol of Sovereignty and power. His vision was that each crenel (the 'battlements' at the top of a castle's outer wall) should be topped with a tall, many-branched silver candelabrum, and on each candelabrum would be placed a silver crown. On the top of the central tower, he envisioned a golden candelabrum topped with a golden crown. At night, each candelabrum would burn with candles whose flame no wind could put out. It is worth pausing for a few moments to recreate this wonderful vision in your mind's eye...

The Kingdom of Sorelois, the character of its ruler Galehaut, and the attributions of its most important castle all challenge you, the Seeker, to think about the nature of Sovereignty and rulership. In this kingdom you are invited to consider the nature of your relationship with the Faery Kingdoms, and above all your relationship with the earth or Planetary Being. On a more immediate level, you are asked to consider how you stand in relationship to your own Self. Do you have rulership over your own thoughts and emotions? Do you shine with a steady, unflickering flame no matter what the circumstances?

In addition to the principles represented by his kingdom, Galehaut himself has three different titles. He is known as 'The Lord of the Faraway Isles,' 'The Uncrowned King,' and 'The Son of the Fair Giantess.' These titles describe the principles and archetypes that he represents, and indicate the challenges he offers to those who enter his kingdom. You can confront each of these challenges by taking the imaginative journeys described below, and observing your reactions and realisations to what you see and experience.

THE FIRST CHALLENGE OF SORELOIS: THE LORD OF THE FARAWAY ISLES

Galehaut's first title can be misleading, and is deliberately so. It acts as a veil or a layer of mist that hides the Kingdom of Sorelois from the eyes of the curious, and its function is to test your *belief* in Faery. It's easy to 'believe' intellectually, in your head, but not in your heart.

Before you begin the following and all subsequent journeys into Faery, place your symbolic Round Table in front of you so that it will serve as a magical talisman.

In your imagination, travel to the chamber of the Round Table. When the chamber has formed clearly in your Inner vision, take your place at the Round Table. Observe and acknowledge those who are seated with you. Then make your contact with Gwenevere. She will not accompany you on your first visit to Sorelois although she will be present at the start and conclusion of your journey in order to offer you any guidance you may need. Take note of anything she says to you in relation to your journey. Observe any others who are seated with you about the Table.

Then turn your attention to the pale golden veil that hangs at the Southern quarter. When you feel ready to start your journey, rise from the table, and stand before the veil. Step into the veil, and allow its colour to permeate your consciousness so that your state of awareness changes.

As your consciousness softens, you will find that the Inner landscape that lies on the other side of the veil begins to brighten into reality and take on form and definition.

When you are ready, step through the veil. You step out into warm sunshine, and a beautiful seascape lies in front of you. You are standing on the top of a grassy cliff overlooking a calm blue sea that stretches to the far horizon. A soft wind, laden with sea-salt, blows gently onto your face.

You are lulled by the sun's warmth and the sound of the gentle waves lapping on the beach far below you. You can hear the faint sound of seabirds calling in the distance. The sun is high over the sea in front of you. Its dazzling light bounces off the blue water, so that each tiny wave and dimple in the sea's surface becomes a glittering, dancing pattern of light. You half-close your eyes against the glare, and the light turns into tiny rainbows between your eyelashes. The golden light is all around you. You slowly breathe it in through your pores … until you feel as if you have become one with the dancing, sparkling light and you have dissolved into light.

After a while, you become aware that on the far horizon, a group of tiny islands has appeared. They are almost lost in the haze; they are faint indigo shadows on the sea. You dreamily try to count them, but they seem to come and go. They seem so Faraway. They are the Faraway Islands.

You wonder why they have appeared, and what their significance is. You know that there is a paradox in their apparent distance from you. If you simply stepped into a boat and sailed towards them, you know that you would never reach them.

You realise that part of their attraction lies in their inaccessibility. As long as they stay on the distant horizon you can longingly dream about the intriguing secrets they might hold, but remain comfortable in the knowledge that they may always be just beyond your reach. They represent the possibility of escape from your own reality into something different, and better. They are something for tomorrow, for when you have enough time to spare, for when you need a diversion to brighten your life.

Think about their distance from you, and of what investment you might have in maintaining this distance. What would happen if you could reach them easily, instantaneously? Think about how this might change your relationship with them...

This concludes your first journey into Sorelois. When you are ready, turn back and see the golden veil hanging before you. Walk into the veil, and give yourself a moment or two to adjust your Inner vision to the chamber of the Round Table on the other side.

Then take your seat at the table. Explain what you have experienced to Gwenevere, and take note of her response.

When you are ready, make a sign of farewell to those who have gathered with you at the Round Table, and return to your own place and time. You can do this by taking the full journey back across the lake, or simply by slowly withdrawing your consciousness from the scene until you are fully back into your physical body.

You have passed the first challenge of Sorelois: *Fear*

The seeming remoteness of the Faraway Islands is an illusion. They are not Faraway, or unattainable, or separated from you by physical space, but by the limits of your own consciousness and the barriers of your belief. All of these Faery Kingdoms can be found wherever and whenever you reach out to them. The distance which lies between you is created, and dissolved, by your own belief. The Faery Kingdom of Sorelois is real: it does not exist on the physical plane but it can be reached wherever you are, simply by raising the level of your conscious awareness. The challenge it presents to you is that you should find the way, in your own heart and mind, to *believe* in its reality. We may want to believe in Faery, and we may think that we believe in Faery, but often we enjoy the intellectual thrill or the imaginative fantasy while making unconscious reservations that hold us back.

It is rare that the full reality of the Faeries and their world becomes open to us in one sudden and complete parting of the veil, and this is just as well. We can only take in a certain amount at a time, especially when moving into the Inner worlds. But because so much of your work with the Faeries involves the use of the creative imagination, it is easy to fall into the trap of half-belief. You have to use your creative imagination in order to reach further into the Faery worlds, but it is then not always easy to be certain that you not are simply inventing what you would like to see. The veils of illusion which lie between us and the Faeries' reality are part of the human condition. We are human, not Faery, and it is not often that we are fortunate enough to be given tangible proof of their existence. The journey towards belief usually happens slowly and gradually.

THE SECOND CHALLENGE OF SORELOIS: THE UNCROWNED KING

Galehaut's second title is 'The Uncrowned King.'

For your second journey to Sorelois, make your preparation as before. If you are working on your own, read the whole journey through beforehand so that you can then recreate it in your mind's eye. When you are ready, travel in your imagination to the chamber of the Round Table.

This time, you find that the chamber is filled with activity! It is lit by bright candles, and the table is laden with food and wine as if for a celebration, an occasion where all can meet together in companionship. Everyone about the table is relaxed and happy, and the air is filled with laughter.

King Arthur and Queen Gwenevere are seated with the others. You are perhaps a little taken aback to see Gwenevere here in this environment; it is a part of her life you have not yet witnessed in your relationship with her. This is the 'Camelot' of popular imagination, filled with the noise and activity of the outer world. You realise something of the task she undertook when she took on human form. You pause for a moment to take this in...

Suddenly, a strange knight, armed from head to toe and carrying a drawn sword, bursts unannounced into the gathering. Without offering any greeting, he strides up to Arthur and Gwenevere and tells them that he has been sent by the Faery Prince Galehaut. Galehaut's message is that Arthur should surrender his kingdom to him! If he does so, the knight tells them, Galehaut will favour him above all the many kings he has so far conquered.

The voices and laughter die away, and a silence descends upon the company.

Arthur rises to his feet, and tells the strange knight that he refuses to accept Galehaut's offer or to be intimidated by his threat.

The knight promptly declares that Galehaut will be in Arthur's land within a month, that he will defeat Arthur in battle and that he will take Gwenevere away with him. He tells the assembled company that Arthur's foolishness will cause nothing but sorrow and misfortune – and then he strides away.

Arthur asks his silent companions if any of them has ever heard of Galehaut. Only one man speaks. He says that he knows Galehaut as young and unmarried, tall, well-loved, noble, gracious and generous, and the successful conqueror of many lands. He adds that it was said that although Galehaut had conquered 30 kingdoms, he had always refused to wear a crown until he ruled Arthur's land of Logres.

The merriment of the evening has been brought to an abrupt close. For a while, you sit and ponder the significance of what has happened. Observe how you feel, and note your thoughts and observations. Observe how Gwenevere reacts to what has taken place.

When you are ready, leave the chamber of the Round Table, and return to your own place and time.

A forthright challenge has been made by the Faery Prince Galehaut to King Arthur and his companions. Until this moment they had felt secure and easy in their circumstances; few of them had even heard of Galehaut and his Faery world. But as we so often discover in the Arthurian legends, the deeper meaning of the story is hidden beneath the outer veneer of circumstances. As is often the case, King Arthur represents humanity and humanity's attitude towards the race of Faeries, and in the scene we have just witnessed, many of those who sat with him in carefree celebration were also representative of humanity, those who had not yet achieved the greater knowledge and understanding that was found within the Order of the Round Table.

In this episode, Galehaut's first challenge to King Arthur, and thus to ourselves, is that we should all, not just a small minority, acknowledge the Faeries' existence.

His second challenge is that we should contemplate the apparently absurd possibility that our world might be 'taken over' by the Faeries.

To King Arthur, the concept that his human world could be ruled by a Faery King was inconceivable. And perhaps you would tend to agree with him? Did you take Galehaut's challenge as a serious threat or did you dismiss this as an imaginary fantasy from the past which has no relevance to the 21st century? What connection did you make with these events?

Our concept of who and what we are, particularly in relation to the earth we inhabit, tends to be firmly embedded in the assumption that the earth is ours and that we are its predominant species. Clearly we are not doing a very good job in demonstrating our responsibilities right now, although we are beginning to realise a little late in the day that the future of the earth lies in our hands. But Galehaut's challenge goes further than simply pointing out how inadequately we are fulfilling our responsibility of care towards the earth, even though this is something that affects the Faeries very much indeed. By asking us to contemplate how it would be if the Faery race was in charge of the earth, he challenges the very assumption that it was ever really 'ours' at all.

The attitude King Arthur conveys to the Faery messenger is representative of humanity in general. He had not heard of the Faery Prince Galehaut and had no intention of taking him seriously. But later in the story, the unthinkable very nearly happens. Galehaut carries out his threat and rides into King Arthur's land with a great army, which fights so fearlessly that it begins to look as if Arthur will be defeated. In fact were it not for the last-minute intervention by a mysterious un-named knight in black armour who comes to Arthur's aid, Arthur would indeed have lost his kingdom to Galehaut.[3] Had this been the case, his human world would have become part of the Faery world, the Faery King Galehaut would have ruled over its human inhabitants, and their lives would have become very different indeed.

But Galehaut's threat is not of an actual, physical overrunning of humanity by the Faeries. His challenge is that we should make a change in our *consciousness*. He asks that we should loosen our fundamental belief in our own precedence on earth. We are challenged to contemplate what it would be like if the human race was not the dominant species on earth. And more than this, we are asked to question whether our belief in our supremacy is simply an illusion.

How do you think the human race stands in comparison with the Faery race? Who is the inheritor of the earth, and who will be its saviour? Who represents the earth?

Contemplate what might have happened if the outcome of Galehaut's challenge had been different and the Faery host had won the day. Do you believe that humankind, or Faerykind, have ultimate responsibility over the earth? Which race is the rightful Sovereign of the Earth?

As you ponder these questions you may begin to find that your awareness of yourself in relation to the Faeries, and the Earth, begins to change.

You have passed the second challenge of Sorelois: *Pride*

THE THIRD CHALLENGE OF SORELOIS: THE SON OF THE FAIR GIANTESS

Galehaut's third title is 'The Son of the Fair Giantess.' As was mentioned earlier, the race of giants was regarded with some hesitancy even at the time when these legends were first recorded, and since then we have moved even further from understanding who or what they were. Regrettably, the modern concept of a giantess is almost always derogatory. Part of the problem is that in Britain, at least, we have never tendered much respect to our ancient Gods and Goddesses and none at all to our giants! We might contrast this perhaps with the Grecian attitude to the Titan giantesses such as Mnemosyne or Themis who retain a dignified presence throughout Greek myth and story, or with Gerd, the beautiful giantess of Norse mythology.

In Sorelois, however, there is no such ambivalence concerning the giantess who is Galehaut's mother and known simply as the Fair Giantess: she is a tall, wondrously beautiful, powerful, golden-haired being, one of our forgotten Goddesses. The ancient power of her race is reflected in Galehaut's own appearance and demeanour. His appearance is of a potent energy and fighting power that is comparable to those of the High Faery race of the Tuatha dé Danaan such as Midir or Óengus Óg.

The beauty and power of the Faeries' appearance can present something of a dilemma to us. The especial vibrancy and potency of Faery energy is almost always an inspiration and delight, but it can become a problem if we allow ourselves to be glamorised by them and fail to see them clearly and objectively. It is quite easy to fall into the belief that Faeries provide an attractive alternative to humans, but it is not wise to neglect your human relationships in favour of Faery relationships or to be seduced into what you think a Faery relationship might offer. Because Faery energy is so strong and clear it is easy to mistake it for human sexual energy. Problems can arise if the attraction we feel towards Faeries becomes a seduction, whether this manifests as a goal to be pursued for the 'fix' it gives, as a feeling of power, sexual desire or fulfilment, a feeling of superiority because you possess secret knowledge, or simply an exciting escape from the tedium of your mundane existence.

The following exercise is designed to encourage you to think about the nature of your own relationship with Faery Beings. Because they are unhampered by a physical body, Faeries have a much closer awareness of energy than humans and a much more developed sense of the subtleties of colour, light and sound that surround them. They do not experience sexual energy as we do: it forms a part of their own relationships but they do not experience lust, sexual jealousy or any of the other difficulties that cloud our human relationships. However, they do delight in exploring human sexual energy purely as an energetic sensation, and when you forge a close relationship with the Faeries you may realise that they are using this as a way of communicating with you. They understand how strongly this particular energy is manifested and experienced by humans, and they like to become involved in exchanging this energy with you as a means of communication and shared experience. You may be surprised to discover that gender plays no part in this!

Make your preparation as before, and travel to the chamber of the Round Table.

This time, although you may be aware that others have joined you, your attention is especially drawn to Galehaut, who is seated next to Gwenevere. Visualise him carefully, building his image as described below. Have in mind the suggested questions, or any others that you may wish to ask, and note the answers and realisations that are given to you.

Galehaut is a Faery warrior of exquisite beauty. He is very tall, and dressed in Faery armour which is of a metal so delicate that it seems almost fluid. It shines with silver, bronze and red-gold light. It is embellished with a complex and fantastical engraved pattern whose intricacy is far beyond the ability of mortal craftsmen.

He carries a tall spear. It too shines brightly, as if it is a part of a continuous slender column of light that reaches far into the sky above, and also travels deep into the earth beneath. It is a conduit for light and inspiration, not a weapon.

Galehaut's hair is golden, and he wears a tall golden filigree crown. His eyes are filled with light. You are aware of his descent from the Fair Giantess, a Goddess of the Earth's remote past, and of how her power flows through him.

Be aware of his Sovereignty. What does this mean to you? How does it affect you?

You realise that he is aware of your presence. Pause in your meditation, and allow sufficient time to make your contact with him on an energetic level…

Observe your thoughts and feelings, note how you relate to him, and how he relates to you.

If you are female, do you find him attractive? Do you find him sexually attractive? How are you dealing with this? Do you feel a desire to explore this type of relationship with him?

If you are male, how do you relate to this male Faery? How are you affected by his appearance? If you are aware of his sexual energy, how do you react to this?

When you are ready, indicate your wish to end the contact. Conclude your meditation and return to your own place and time.

There is no doubt that a relationship with a Faery can bring great reward, not only personally but in the greater sphere of mutual understanding that has ultimate relevance for the whole of Faery, humanity and the Planetary Being. But just as in any relationship between one human and another, the ultimate aim in a relationship between Faery and human should be a basis of love and respect which recognises the other for who they are. We should not assume that every Faery who makes our acquaintance is doing so for reasons that we would regard as acceptable. Faeries can be very curious of humans and will not always be as sensitive or empathetic of your feelings as you might expect. In fact many of our most frequently experienced feelings such as tenderness, sentimentality, guilt, jealousy, irritation, impatience, greed, depression, loneliness and so on, are not experienced by Faeries. For the most part, they experience the higher emotions rather than the lower feelings just described: emotions such as joy, delight, love, bliss, ecstasy – in fact all those emotions that we tend to experience only through sex, religious fervour or use of recreational drugs!

Those of the Faery world whom you meet in these pages and who play a part in the Mysteries of the Round Table are those who have elected to work with humankind. They are ambassadors, able and willing to communicate with us, and for the most part they tend to be those who appear in a form recognisably similar in appearance to humans. But Faeries are not all good looking, and there are many of their kind who may seem ugly or grotesque to your eyes. If you meet such Faeries on your travels, don't judge them by their appearance.

You have passed the third test of Sorelois: *Glamour*

THE GIFTS OF THE FAERY KINGDOM OF SORELOIS

The final journey in this chapter takes you into the heart of Sorelois, where you will encounter Galehaut and Gwenevere as its King and Queen. Here, you will be able to experience for yourself some of the power and responsibility of Sovereignty within a Faery realm. The story is summarised below.[4]

King Arthur is at court with Gwenevere and his knights and ladies. A beautiful maiden arrives in their midst, accompanied by an escort of thirty or more knights and men at arms. She is richly dressed in a silken robe and cloak, and her hair falls down her back in one long, thick braid. Everyone makes way for her, as she is obviously of noble birth. But they are astonished when she announces loudly and boldly that she has been sent by Queen Gwenevere, the daughter of King Leodegrance. This makes no sense: Gwenevere is sitting with King Arthur.

The maiden looks at all those gathered about her, and appears to recognise an old, white-haired knight who is holding a golden box set with precious stones. When she catches his eye, he steps forward and hands the box to her. She opens it, and takes from it a letter hung with a golden seal. She asks that everyone in the court should be brought together so that they will be able to hear her read the letter. When everyone has assembled, a clerk reads the letter aloud. But when he realises what it contains, tears of grief begin to roll down his cheeks.

The letter is from a lady who claims to be the 'real' Gwenevere! She claims that King Arthur is living with an imposter. She claims that it was *she* who had been married to King Arthur in the Church of Saint Stephen, but after having spent only one night with him she had been taken away and cast out, and the other Gwenevere had been put in her place. The 'substitute' Gwenevere, the letter claims, had ever since plotted to torment her and cause her death.[5] But she was now ready to resume her rightful place as Arthur's Queen, and she demanded that Arthur should publicly recognise her as such by removing the other Gwenevere from his side and having her tried for treason. If Arthur did not agree, she would forbid him to retain possession of the Round Table. It must be returned to her at once; none of the knights of the Round Table should ever use that title again, and no representation of the Round Table should henceforward be used in his court. (It is interesting to note that the ownership and future of the Round Table and the Order of knights associated with it seem to be of as much importance to the 'false' Gwenevere as is her wish to be seen as Arthur's Queen.)

Although the contents of the letter were initially received with shocked disbelief, as the days and weeks went past Arthur became increasingly convinced by the claim. So much so, that when the 'false' Gwenevere eventually arrived at his court in person, he took her for his wife with great enthusiasm and made clear his intent that his real wife should be imprisoned and tried for treason just as she had demanded.

But Galehaut had already promised to Gwenevere that if such an event should ever come to pass, he would provide a safe haven for her by giving her his kingdom of Sorelois, where she could stay for as long as she needed. When Galehaut saw that King Arthur had been taken in by the false Gwenevere he lost no time in making good his promise. He took Gwenevere into his kingdom, gave his land into her possession, and saw to it that his people gave her their oath of loyalty.

Nearly three years passed in this fashion. Eventually, the false Gwenevere was found to be near to death from an apparent overdose of the herbal potions which seemed necessary to sustain her existence. She confessed to her crime and died, rather horribly. Arthur was persuaded to ask Gwenevere's forgiveness, and she returned from Sorelois to resume her place within the court of the Round Table.

But during the three years she had spent in Sorelois, Arthur's kingdom became a Wasteland. By allowing himself to be seduced by the glamour of the false Gwenevere he had failed to exercise proper Sovereignty over his own Self and those about him. His Kingdom no longer had a Faery Queen, and the bridge of communication between human and Faery which was maintained while the true Gwenevere was at his side, was broken. Without the Faery Queen at the court of the Round Table the land had become barren. Here is another example of the Waste Land that we first encountered in Boron's description of the journey of the Grail from the Holy Land to Avalon.

BECOMING A SOVEREIGN: WEARING THE FAERY CROWN

The final journey to Sorelois takes you to the heart of this Faery kingdom, where you will enter Galehaut's castle the Proud Fortress. The journey enables you to experience for yourself the concept of Sovereignty, in relation to both the human and Faery worlds.

Make your preparation as usual, and journey in vision to the chamber of the Round Table.

This time, Galehaut and Gwenevere are not present: they are waiting to receive you in Sorelois. When you are ready, turn to the golden veil at the Southern quarter, and stand before it. Then walk into the veil, and pause within its colour to allow the scene behind you to fade, and the land of Sorelois to open up before you.

At first, you can see only the gentle outline of green rolling hills, softened by a purple haze. There is stillness and peace over all the land. In the far distance, you can see a castle, built entirely of shining silver and gold. The shape of the castle looks very like a crown. This is the Proud Fortress, the heart and centre of Sorelois.

It is set on a high cliff, above what looks like a fast-running river. Yet this is not a river of water, but of a flowing energy that acts in polarity with the circling, spiralling energy of the castle.[6]

You realise that to reach the castle does not involve physical effort of movement across a measurable distance, but a change of consciousness. You can best achieve this change of consciousness by deliberately focusing on the details of the appearance of the castle and observing them in increasing detail and clarity. This is a good opportunity to use your skills of seeing Faery colours.

From where you stand, first look at the river flowing at its foot, and notice its straight, fast moving, clear energy. Note its relationship with the energy of the castle, and its connection with the energy of the surrounding land.

Then, look at the outer wall or ring of the castle. Focus on it until it becomes clear and bright in your mind's eye. It has a silvery, reflective, smooth surface. It is not made of any earthly substance but is an organisation of energy. This 'wall' is formed of etheric energy, and is an expression of the Inner tides and cycles of movement that support the physical world. The etheric tides are revealed within the castle's outer wall as a turning, spiralling movement.

The top of this outer wall is crenellated, but these Faery 'crenels' are whorls or tongues of silver flame that are released from the spiralling energy of the walls and dissolve into tiny points of silver light, like candle-flames floating freely into the air. In this way, the energy of the castle is broadcast into the kingdom that surrounds it.

Now focus on the central tower. It is golden, and shines with a light that radiates from within. As you focus your attention on it, the light increases. The top of the tower seems almost to have dissolved in the light but you can see flames flickering gently about its rim, and a column of pale golden light rises from the tower, high into the sky.

You would like to experience the castle closer at hand, and because you are in a Faery Kingdom you can achieve this simply by desiring that it should be so, and focusing on your intention. You move towards it effortlessly.

You arrive at the flowing river, and cross over it, noting its energy as you do so. You move effortlessly up the steep cliff, and through the shining silver outer wall of the castle, experiencing its energy. You arrive at the golden, inner tower. You move effortlessly through its golden walls. You are now within the central enclosure.

You have arrived at the heart of Sorelois. Here, you find Gwenevere and Galehaut. They are each seated on a golden throne. They each wear a crown that is an exact replica in miniature of the castle: an outer rim of silver and an inner rim of gold. Tiny flames of silver and gold drift upwards from the crowns.

Both Gwenevere and Galehaut are bathed in the golden light that fills this heart of Sorelois. You realise how closely their consciousness is connected with the castle and with the entire kingdom that lies around them.

When you have made your contact with Gwenevere, ask her if you may experience for yourself what it means to be Queen of this land. If you receive her consent, you will find that she rises from her throne and indicates that you should take her place upon the throne for a short while. When you are seated, she removes the crown from her head and gently places it on yours.

If you prefer, you can undertake this same exercise with Galehaut.

Allow yourself sufficient time to experience all of this. Experience what it feels like to wear the crown. Realise the connection between the crown, your consciousness, and the castle. Then extend your awareness beyond the castle to the land all about it. What is your connection to this Faery kingdom, and what is your responsibility towards it while you are seated at its centre?

Finally, if you can, extend your awareness to the human land of Logres, and look at it from your throne at the heart of this Faery kingdom.

While Gwenevere was in Sorelois, Logres became a Wasteland. What are your thoughts and realisations as to why this happened? And how could the situation best be remedied?

When you are ready, carefully return the crown and relinquish your seat.

Return to the chamber of the Round Table by moving back through the golden and silver walls, across the purple haze that covers the green land of Sorelois, and through the golden veil.

Take your seat at the Round Table and share your experiences with those who have joined you. Return carefully to your own place and time.

This experience of Sorelois' gift of the experience of Sovereignty concludes your work within this kingdom. You may of course return to it as often as you wish: there is always more to discover. Each time you share your knowledge and experiences with those who join you at the Round Table you will become more actively involved in building bridges between human and Faery for others to follow.

1   The story of Gwenevere, Galehaut and the Faery Kingdom of Sorelois can be found in: ed. Norris J. Lacy, *The Lancelot-Grail Reader* (New York, Garland Publishing Inc., 2000)

2   The word Logres is derived from the Welsh word *Lloegr*, which means 'England.'

3   The mysterious Black Knight is later revealed to be Lancelot.

4   If you would like to read it in full it appears in the *Lancelot-Grail Reader* p.143ff

5   According to the story told in the *Lancelot-Grail* there were indeed two Gweneveres, both daughters of Leodegrance, although the mother of the false Gwenevere was the wife of one of his servants. The story can be found in *Lancelot-Grail Reader* pp.76-77. The real Gwenevere could be distinguished by the mark of a crown on her back. The episode is discussed more fully in *Red Tree, White Tree.*

6   This combination of circle and straight line can often be observed by plotting out ley lines on an Ordnance Survey map together with the ancient structures that delineate them. Frequently, an ancient castle or hill fort is found in conjunction with a long straight ley line that glances across its perimeter as if it were a stick spinning a whirling top. Faery castles can often be found on Ordnance Survey maps!

CHAPTER SIX

The Faery Kingdom of Gorre

THE SECOND OF THE Faery Kingdoms associated with Gwenevere is the Kingdom of Gorre. The gateway into Gorre lies in the western quarter of the chamber of the Round Table.

The description of Gwenevere's connection with Gorre is found in the Arthurian story known as 'The Knight of the Cart.' If you would like to read the story in full, it is one of a group of Arthurian romances written by the French author Chrétien de Troyes at the end of the 12th century.[1] The main events of the story and the magical theory that lies behind them are discussed in full in *Red Tree, White Tree*, and you might find this useful preparatory reading before you approach the practical work in the following pages.

The journey into Gorre constitutes a magical ritual initiation into Faery. The initiation was originally taken by Lancelot, who travelled into Gorre in order to find Gwenevere who had been 'abducted' there by the Faery Prince Meleagant. Having experienced the lessons and challenges of Gorre, Lancelot is now able to guide others who follow his footsteps. In this chapter you will be taken through each separate part of the magical journey as it appears in the original story, and at each stage it will be made clear what is being asked of you, as the initiate of this ritual journey.

In Chapter Seven, you will find that the complete journey has been set out as a magical ritual for you to perform. You can undertake it with a group, or with a partner, or on your own within your imagination, but it will hold a great deal more meaning for you if you have worked through the current chapter first!

MAGICAL CORRESPONDENCES OF THE KINGDOM OF GORRE	
Direction:	West
Symbol:	A five-pointed star
Challenge:	Dedication
Gift:	Initiation
Initiators:	Gwenevere, Meleagant

In Sorelois, you were asked to examine any fears you might hold in your approach to Faery; you were challenged to examine your beliefs about the relative status of human and Faery within the world, and you were asked to be aware of the dangers of glamour, enchantment and pride in your relationship with Faery. In any School of the Mysteries, the initiate will be led through just such a series of tests and challenges, not to create difficulties just for the sake of it but because when you work with beings of another level of creation you need to properly understand what you are doing. The kingdom of Gorre lies further away than Sorelois; it is more difficult to find, and its challenges work at a deeper level. The further you travel into the Inner worlds, the more responsible you must become. When you begin to engage more directly with the forces and forms of the Inner levels of creation you will begin to have an effect on what happens to others as well as yourself, so the responsibilities become greater.

So with this in mind, let us move straight into the story! In essence, it is very simple, and can be summarised as follows:

Gorre is ruled by the Faery King Bademagus and his son Meleagant. Meleagant comes to the court of the Round Table and throws down a challenge to King Arthur and his knights, taunting them by saying that he holds many human prisoners in Gorre. He says that he might perhaps agree to release them, but only if one of Arthur's knights agrees to fight a duel with him in defence of Gwenevere. Meleagant specifies that the duel should take place in a nearby forest. Arthur agrees to the challenge in principle, but sends Lancelot to fight the duel on his behalf. Meleagant leaves the court, taking Gwenevere with him.

As with the story of Galehaut and the Faery kingdom of Sorelois, we find again that the main characters seem to know what is going to happen, a sure indication of the story's origin as a magical ritual.

In this instance, Lancelot had previously been advised by the Lady of the Lake that these events were about to take place and had been instructed by her to follow Gwenevere into Gorre and bring her back. He set out after them, accompanied by Gawain. But once he reached the forest, he encountered a series of unexpected tests and challenges which delayed him so much that he was unable to catch up with them. When he finally reached Gorre he was challenged even more strongly, this time by Gwenevere herself. But eventually they both returned safely to King Arthur's court.

There are several distinct stages to the journey of initiation within this apparently simple story, and they are described below. You might like to read through all of them straight away in order to get an overall picture of what lies ahead, but you should then work through them one by one, taking as much time as you need in order to complete each stage to your satisfaction.

THE CALL FROM THE LADY OF THE LAKE

The journey into Gorre is initiated by the Lady of the Lake, and her role in this story is of considerable significance. The Lady is not always named, although in later versions of the legends she is called Vivien, Niniane, Nimué or variants of the same. It may well be that her title refers to a role or position of authority within these Mysteries rather than to a single person. She has a special and very positive relationship with Lancelot, having been responsible for raising and educating him. Indeed, he is often called Lancelot of the Lake for this very reason.

The Lady of the Lake remains an enigmatic figure in the Arthurian stories and her enduring influence is far greater than can be explained by her infrequent appearances and sometimes puzzling behaviour. Almost everyone who has heard of the legends of King Arthur and the knights of the Round Table has also heard of the Lady of the Lake, but our image of her tends to be based almost entirely on the single episode in which King Arthur, who had broken his original sword (the one he had pulled from the stone) was guided to her by Merlin in order that she could provide him with a replacement. The iconic image of a white silk-clad arm emerging from the depths of a lake and brandishing the sword Excalibur takes a powerful hold in our imagination.

But alongside Gwenevere, the Lady of the Lake is one of the foremost of the teachers of the wisdom of the Round Table. It is her continuing work in this role from the Inner planes that explains the powerful presence she still retains in our consciousness despite her seemingly minor role in the stories. Merlin teaches primarily in the Outer Court of the Round Table by demonstrating the powers of the elements and providing the Elemental Initiations that form the first stage of the knights' progress. Gwenevere works within the main company of the knights of the Round Table and offers them direct experience of the Faery worlds through her practice of repeatedly moving between the human and Faery worlds. But the Lady of the Lake works directly with the *minds* of her pupils, by teaching them how to make the necessary changes of consciousness in order to perceive the Inner worlds. Whenever she makes an appearance in the human world, whether this is to the knights of legend or the Seekers of the 21st century, her purpose is to initiate and stimulate a change in consciousness that leads to a greater understanding of the dynamics of the Inner worlds of creation and our relationship with them.[2]

As we found in connection with the Faery Kingdoms, there is not a great deal to be gained by attempting to connect the Lady of the Lake with any actual lake. Her lake is not a specific or identifiable stretch of water although inevitably some lakes have become especially associated with her. She can be contacted by sitting quietly and in a receptive frame of mind on the shore of almost any stretch of flat, calm, inland water. (But she is not a Sea Priestess: she cannot be contacted through the power of the ocean or the ebb and flow of the sea tides.)

One of the foremost ways in which she teaches her pupils is by using the image and colours of the lake itself as a magical tool. In fact rather than being *of* the Lake it might be more accurate to say that the Lady herself *is* the Lake. She embodies the qualities of deep, calm water that acts as a mirror to the Inner worlds and demonstrates the state of mind you need to have attained in order to reach them. You can experience how this works right away by closing your eyes and visualising a wide expanse of still, dark blue water with a mirror-like surface...

You will probably have noticed that simply imagining a lake caused you to relax a little and to breathe more slowly and deeply. When you do this, your inner awareness is sure to open up as you become more physically relaxed and your consciousness is released from the demands of the everyday world. Blue is calming to the emotions but, paradoxically, it is stimulating to the mind, which is why it can be difficult to sleep if you have spent the evening staring at a computer or television screen.

We can take the concept of the lake further by saying that not only does the Lady represent the lake but the lake itself is a symbol of the mind and the different states of consciousness that can be entered through the use of the mind and imagination. The lake therefore represents the prime arena of magical work and it is used by the Lady as a practical, working tool, a means by which she can teach her pupils how to develop and extend their perception of the Inner worlds. The lake represents the magical mirror of our mind and imagination, through which we can receive, understand and reflect the Inner worlds. It must be kept clear and still by the practice of meditation, unruffled by the turbulence of emotional issues, deepened through knowledge and wisdom and capable of extension into the vast waters of the cosmos.

In Chapter Three you developed your awareness of colour in the Faery worlds by exploring the Innerworld properties of the colours red, orange, yellow and green. As preparation for the more advanced work represented by the kingdom of Gorre, here is a further series of magical exercises designed to help you increase your awareness of the Inner worlds by working with the colours of the lake: blue, indigo and violet. Just as you worked with the first four colours of the visible spectrum by observing the colours around you in the mundane world and then working with the qualities of the colours in the Faery realm, so this pattern continues with the remaining three.

THE COLOURS OF THE LAKE: BLUE, INDIGO AND VIOLET

If you look around you at this very moment you will probably see blue everywhere. It is a very versatile colour, and unlike the colours of the lower end of the spectrum it can be used in almost every situation. It does not make a bold statement and is perhaps the least memorable of all colours. Except for some of the harsher modern pigments, blue fades into the background.

Herein lies its secret: as it recedes into the background so it subtly draws your attention with it, away from the mundane levels of reality. When you are working with the Inner properties of colour, blue acts as a gateway into deeper states of consciousness through its remarkable ability to quieten the emotions while at the same time supporting a clear and lively state of consciousness. Faery blue tends to be cold, almost metallic; it is the colour of Faery armour. And in the Faery realms blue also acts as a mirror to the glittering, shining qualities of star-light.

Indigo is a strange colour and not always easy to bring to mind. If you try to find an example of the use of indigo in the world about you or if you try to picture it in your mind's eye the chances are that you will not find it easy to settle on an exact shade. Some don't consider it to be a separate colour at all, just a variation of blue or violet. However, indigo does possess properties that are not found in either blue or violet and the very process of searching for its exact hue brings about an opening up of consciousness into levels beyond the physical. Perhaps it is best considered as a 'vibration' rather than a colour. It is loved by the Faeries for its depth of resonance. Indigo is the Faery black!

Finally, violet, which is not an easy colour to reproduce in the physical world and often looks sickly or cheap. With this final colour of the visible spectrum even our language becomes imprecise. Our violet flower is not the same colour as the violet of the rainbow, and Faery violet is even purer, and paler. It is as if the colour violet is already partially an Inner plane colour, and we can only see an approximation of its true vibration as it recedes into palest violet, and then beyond the visible spectrum into ultra-violet. Ultra-violet is harmful to human eyesight, but it can be a useful exercise to try to *imagine* it, and you will find that it is a very stimulating colour in the Inner worlds.

When Lancelot first heard the call of the Lady of the Lake, he had taken himself away from the court of the Round Table and was living in solitude in the countryside near Tintagel. You do not need to live in the wilds in order to make contact with the Lady of the Lake although you are unlikely to hear her voice above the clamour of city life. But the following exercises will help you to reach her in meditation, and become open to her guidance.

WORKING WITH INNER BLUE

In meditation, imagine that you are standing on the shore of the circular lake that you visualise when you are journeying to the chamber of the Round Table. But this time, there is no boat, no mist and no island. The smooth, flat surface of the lake is calm, unruffled, and a beautiful deep blue. There is no activity.

Attune your mind to the lake and become at one with its properties. Adjust your consciousness to the frequency of blue and notice how your breathing slows and your Inner awareness begins to expand.

Focus solely on the lake. Do not look for symbols or hidden meaning but simply concentrate on retaining the steady image of the calm, flat, expanse of water. Keep the lake, and your consciousness, wide, receptive and empty. Focus on visualising the colour blue, and on maintaining the smooth, empty surface of the lake. Realise the connection between your emotional state, and the appearance of the lake. If you are feeling ruffled about something, focusing your attention on the calm lake will help you to become calm in yourself. You will find that the natural tendency is for the lake to expand in circumference as you become calmer, and you should allow this to happen. Be aware of how your consciousness expands with the boundaries of the lake. *The lake and your consciousness are one.*

When you are ready, allow yourself to realise the presence of the Lady of the Lake standing on the shore. Simply allow her presence to manifest near to you. Although it often works well to attempt to make contact with an Inner plane being by visualising an appropriate form for them to adopt, this method does not best suit the Lady of the Lake. Her very nature is fluid and changeable, and she is likely to appear in many different forms. The best way to make your contact with her is to send out your desire to meet with her, and then allow her to appear to you in whatever form she chooses. She might choose a conventional image, but don't be surprised if she does not.

When you have made your contact with her, return your attention to the calm surface of the lake, and you may find that a symbol arises from its depths. Allow it to do so naturally and of its own accord; don't deliberately seek a symbol or gift from the Lady. Keep this meditation, and your consciousness, as calm, pure and *empty* as you are able. If a symbol or an idea is given to you, accept it just as Arthur took his sword, and take it back with you into your daily life. Work with it and observe what meaning unfolds from it as it develops in your daily life. But don't be tempted to gather a bottom drawer full of symbols – one good symbol lasts a long time!

WORKING WITH INNER INDIGO

When you have worked with the Inner properties of blue to your satisfaction, move on to the second meditation. You might like to undertake this exercise in several stages. Return to the lake and stand on the shore, but this time, visualise the colour of the lake gradually changing from blue to indigo.

Notice how the lake and your consciousness shift in vibration as the colour changes.

Now gently push out the boundaries of the lake until it is as wide as you can imagine. Keep extending the perimeter of the lake in your consciousness until it is so vast that you can no longer measure its size and until it reaches the boundaries of your vision. Hold this image steady in your mind's eye. Realise that the vast circular lake is actually the circle of the universe. Take a while to contemplate this. The apparent size of the universe, and your consciousness, are related. As the lake expands, so does your consciousness.

When you are ready, become aware of the depth of the lake, and allow your consciousness to plumb its depths. In your mind's eye, reach down, as far as feels comfortable to you, into its indigo waters.

And now realise that the deep lake forms a mirror to the stars. The depths of the lake form the lower half of a great sphere; the starry sky forms the upper half of the sphere.

Allow your consciousness to reach into the stars, above and below.

Conclude your meditation by allowing the lake to retract to its original smaller size. This will have the effect of closing down your Inner awareness.

When you are ready, return to full waking consciousness.

WORKING WITH INNER VIOLET

The third stage of work with the Lady of the Lake takes you further into the spiritual worlds. This exercise is shorter and more powerful.

Return to the lake, and stand on the shore. Visualise the lake as before, calm and still, but this time visualise its waters gradually becoming filled with pale violet light. Allow this light to fill the lake, and to fill your consciousness. Hold this steady for as long as you are able.

Observe what effect this has on your consciousness.

Then, hold in your mind the realisation that the Lady of the Lake, Gwenevere, and all the women, human or Faery, who are found within the Arthurian and Grail legends, are servers of the Great Goddess.

When you are ready, allow yourself to be receptive to whatever vision of the Goddess is given to you within the violet light. Take your time over this.

Conclude your meditation by returning gradually to normal waking consciousness. We can now return to the story of the magical journey into Gorre with the increased Inner awareness that has been brought about through the guidance and inspiration of the Lady of the Lake.

The Lady has some difficulty in finding Lancelot, and discovers him in a state of distress. He is living in the wilds near Tintagel, far from the court of the Round Table and his companions. He has reached the stage of spiritual development in which the things of the world have lost their attraction and even the magical life of the court of the Round Table has become meaningless. He has retreated into the wilds of nature in order to find his way forward and although he may not realise it at the time, the Lady is about to provide him with the opportunity he is looking for.

She tells him that he should go to the court of the Round Table where he will discover that Gwenevere is about to be taken away by Meleagant, but adds enigmatically that he will not be able to prevent this from happening. Lancelot does as he has been instructed.

THE JOURNEY INTO GORRE: KNOWING YOUR HEART'S DESIRE

Lancelot loves Gwenevere, so this would seem reason enough that he should try to rescue her from apparent capture and imprisonment. If he had no desire for her he would have been unlikely to have ventured on such a journey. But Gorre is not a prison, it is a Faery Kingdom. Gwenevere is a willing participant in this ritual of initiation; she had not been captured, and she could return whenever she wished. In Lancelot's journey of initiation into Faery, her purpose is to guide him to a greater understanding of the Faery Mysteries. The real purpose of Lancelot's journey into Gorre is not to bring Gwenevere back into the human world and return her to King Arthur, but that he should achieve a level of consciousness where he might understand more of the higher purpose of the human and Faery races and their shared destiny.

What is your heart's desire at the present moment? What was it ten years ago? What do you imagine it will be in ten years' time? What spurs you on in your quest into the Inner worlds?

THE JOURNEY INTO GORRE: THE DWELLER ON THE THRESHOLD

Lancelot follows Meleagant and Gwenevere as they travel through a dark forest, but does not catch up with them. He eventually arrives at a castle. He is persuaded by the occupants of the castle to spend the night there, and is offered a choice of three beds which are placed side by side in a large hall. He chooses the middle of the three and settles down into sleep. During the night, a spear descends from the roof, bursts into flames and strikes him on his left side. He puts out the flames, grabs the spear, and hurls it away from him.

The challenges encountered by Lancelot in the castle in the forest represent an important element of the journey of initiation. Lancelot has to make a choice between three options that are open to him at this stage of his progress, and by doing so he is offered the opportunity to confront his shadow, represented here by the flaming spear that threatens his life.

The phrase 'Dweller on the Threshold' is often quoted in esoteric work although it was probably coined comparatively recently.[3] Sooner or later every Seeker of the Mysteries must confront his or her shadow, and this process should be well underway before you embark on the deeper levels of magical work or it will become fuelled by magical power and turn into more than you might have bargained for.

The confrontation with the Dweller on the Threshold describes a process which has always been a vital stage of the Seeker's journey, although the ways in which the Dweller has been described vary according to the psychological and spiritual make-up of the individual or society in question. The Dweller has been envisaged as a gigantic, hideous monster capable of physical or psychic attack on the Seeker, though it is more appropriate to think of the process of coming to terms with it as a manageable and gradual chipping away, not an overwhelming or frightening battle.

You can get a good idea of the nature of your shadow simply by observing what it is in other people that irritates you most. The chances are that you are looking at some unresolved issues that you don't admit to. Confronting your shadow means taking full responsibility for your own actions and the whole of your Self, not just the bits that look good.

Much of this can be seen once again in the ancient separation between human and Faery. Whether we think of the 'Fall' as a fall from grace and innocence or a necessary and inevitable part of the process of taking on the clothing of physicality, the part of us that has come to be referred to as the shadow came about during this process of separation. The instincts of 'fight or flight' that developed at this time, manifest primarily as anger or fear, each of which in essence is a useful and sometimes life-preserving reaction. The problem is that they become distorted into the more 'civilised' and sophisticated patterns of jealousy, resentment, revenge, greed and so on. It is these tendencies, rather than the original instincts, that are hard for us to come to terms with.

These human habits are especially important to be aware of when working with Faeries because they are not experienced by Faeries, who therefore do not understand them.

To demonstrate this very challenge, Lancelot was given a choice of three beds, and three choices. The first bed represented the path of false pride, which is demonstrated by those who insist on being 'human and proud of it' within the Faery world and acting inappropriately. The careless introduction of the qualities of the human shadow into Faery is not the right approach.

The second choice is to deny the shadow which is an inescapable part of being human, and to enter Faery as if you were one of them. This won't work either, because ultimately the Faeries must learn and understand what is involved in being human. Nothing will be achieved if you deny your humanity.

The third choice is the middle way of love, in which you act appropriately within the world of Faery by acknowledging all parts of yourself *with compassion*. If you are able to stand with a Faery (and, of course, with another human being) and be fully yourself, without fear, shame or repression, then you will have achieved a great deal.

Lancelot chose the third option. When he was given the opportunity to confront his shadow he did so with courage and common sense: he was not overwhelmed by the flaming spear and he was able to continue into Faery.

THE JOURNEY INTO GORRE: CROSSING THE RIVER

Lancelot continued to follow Gwenevere and Meleagant through the forest. Sometimes he glimpsed them in the distance, but he could not catch up with them.

Eventually he arrived at the bank of the great river which formed the boundary of the Kingdom of Gorre, whose greatest city, Gorrun, was now visible to him on the far side. There were three possible ways of crossing the river: a Sword Bridge, a Stone Passage and an Underwater Bridge. Lancelot chose to cross the river by the dangerous Sword Bridge, and finally entered Gorre.

He reached the castle of the Faery King Bademagus, where Gwenevere was staying. She came out from the castle to greet him. But she told him that he had wasted his time in coming to find her and she wasn't in the least bit grateful! She left him, and returned to her chamber.

The three ways of approach to Gorre are a more challenging version of the test of the Three Beds. The Stone Passage symbolises the element of earth. It tempts the Seeker to abandon the spiritual quest and return to the material things of the outer world.

The Underwater Passage offers an apparently more easy option but, being underwater, its apparent attractions are an illusion; it is not what it seems, and does not offer any lasting benefit or stability.

The Sword Bridge, although narrow and difficult to cross, represents the only real way forward.

Once he had safely crossed the bridge into Gorre, Lancelot was tested even more strongly, and this time by Gwenevere herself. She made it clear that if he had expected any gratitude or personal reward for managing to reach her, he would be very disappointed. This is a harsh reminder to Lancelot, as to all those who follow his footsteps, that his journey into Faery should not be undertaken through any feelings he might have had for Gwenevere personally. This device of metaphorically sweeping the rug from under the feet of the initiate is used in many Mystery traditions. At the point at which the initiate believes that he is about to be given access into the Inner Sanctum of the Mysteries where all will be finally revealed, he is told that 'There is no God' and it has all been an illusion.

In order to experience something of this challenge for yourself, imagine that you have learnt, from an authority you rely on, that there is absolute proof that the Faery race does not exist and that your belief in them all this time has simply been a delusion. You have invented them because you need to believe in them. How would you react to this?

THE JOURNEY INTO GORRE: THE GARDEN OF PARADISE

Once Lancelot has come to terms with what she has told him, Gwenevere says that he can come to her that night, in her bedchamber in a tower at the centre of the castle. But in order to reach her, Lancelot has to find his way through a garden surrounded by a high wall. When he reaches the tower in which Gwenevere's chamber is situated, he has to remove the iron bars which form a barrier in front of her window before he can climb inside.

With this episode, we arrive at the heart of the initiatory journey into Gorre. The garden through which Lancelot has to pass in order to reach Gwenevere represents the garden of the perfect 'unfallen' world that is described in the bible as the Garden of Eden. Before the human and Faery races separated, they existed side by side in a world which had not taken its final plunge into physicality.[4] By retreating to her chamber at the centre of the castle Gwenevere is moving up in the Inner levels of creation from the Faery Kingdom of Gorre into a higher level, where the Garden of Paradise still exists. In order to reach her, Lancelot must also find his way back into the Garden, where human and Faery are as one. In the Garden, neither Faery nor human is a guest in each other's world but share the same realm of existence. The wall about the garden does not represent an insurmountable obstacle. It is maintained by the belief that the Garden is now barred to us as Adam's descendents. But it serves a valid purpose: it keeps out those who are not yet ready to make this return in their consciousness and belief, just as Adam was prevented from returning to the Garden by the flaming sword which was set across its entrance. If you believe that you are ready to experience this return to the condition of Paradise, the wall will begin to dissolve just as any self-imposed barrier or defence dissolves when it no longer serves a purpose.

If we refer again to Boron's story of the Grail, the Garden of Eden is represented by the early stage of the Grail's journey, before the two groups in Joseph of Arimathea's company grew apart. The work of the Round Table is not separate to the legends of the Grail but an essential preparation for finding it and understanding what it means, and in Gorre we take a big step forward in our journey towards the Grail.

It is significant that we are told that the wall to the garden is crumbling. This is an encouraging sign that the beliefs which once kept Adam, Eve and their Faery brethren out of Paradise are not as rigidly maintained as we might have thought. The potential to reach back into the state of existence symbolised by the Garden is always present. In like manner, the iron bars which surround Gwenevere's window do not represent an insurmountable barrier: Lancelot managed to remove them without much difficulty – and replaced them as he left!

Those familiar with the Qabala and the glyph of the Tree of Life will recognise in this episode the symbolism of the 13th Path that runs from Tiphareth to Kether. In this instance, Gorre represents Tiphareth. After leaving the court of the Round Table in Malkuth, Lancelot would have entered Tiphareth from Yesod, the mysterious forest between the worlds. He then continued up the Middle Pillar along the 13th Path from Tiphareth towards Gwenevere's chamber which represents Daath. The Sephirah of Daath is often likened to an empty room or condemned cell that contains a high, barred window. The conventions of the time and the need to hide the deeper meaning from the casual reader would explain why the story suggests that union with Gwenevere was the ultimate aim of Lancelot's journey. But Qabalists would recognise that his encounter with Gwenevere as Priestess of these Mysteries was an indication that he was moving onwards towards union with the Divine, in the Sephirah of Kether, as the High Priestess is the Tarot card of the 13th Path.

THE RETURN TO THE OUTER WORLD

Although Lancelot spends a night with Gwenevere within her chamber, their outward circumstances do not appear to change. The human prisoners in Gorre who at the beginning of the story were apparently so significant, now fade from the scene. Indeed in Chrétien's telling of the story they are even heard to complain that Lancelot has compromised their security by opening up the way across the Sword Bridge! Meleagant and Lancelot meet and fight several duels, but eventually agree to accept that they have unfinished business which they vow to continue at a later date. Gwenevere leaves Gorre, but not with Lancelot. She returns safely to the court of the Round Table.

If we judge the story by the criteria of the outer world it appears to end on a rather unsatisfactory note. Gwenevere, who was not at any time actually imprisoned in Gorre, returns to Arthur's court of her own free will, as indeed she could have done at any time. Lancelot has apparently gained nothing at all for his efforts, and it looks as if Meleagant will continue to visit Arthur's court and throw down his same challenge for an indefinite time to come.

But this is a magical ritual, not a fairy tale, and within the terms of the magical ritual all makes perfect sense. Gwenevere's purpose in drawing Lancelot into the higher levels of consciousness symbolised by her chamber in the castle has been fulfilled. Lancelot has also achieved the purpose of his journey, which was to reach these levels of consciousness. He too returns to the human world, where he can now guide those who wish to follow him in his journey of initiation. But many will need to follow in his footsteps until an effective magical change has been achieved, so Meleagant will continue to challenge likely candidates until this task is done.

This just leaves us with the prisoners! They are said to be human beings who have been imprisoned by the Faery rulers of Gorre. Again, this does not make sense on a rational level because Faeries cannot imprison humans in their astral world. But if we consider this as another indication of different levels of consciousness, it becomes a comment on the state of mind of those humans who have successfully journeyed into the Faery realm but have not returned fully into their own place and time. Some of them are happy to have opted out of normal human life and retreated into illusion, and resent any attempt to bring them back. This is a useful reminder of the importance of affirming your own humanity and ensuring that you return fully into your own physical body at the end of any meditation or imaginative journey into Faery.

1   There are several available editions of Chrétien's Arthurian romances, but the one used here is Chrétien de Troyes, trans. D.D.R. Owen, *Arthurian Romances* (London, Everyman, 1986)
2   The Lady of the Lake's function within the court of the Round Table can also be thought of in terms of Yin and Yang: the concept that all created life is governed by opposing but complementary forces. If this is applied to the knights of the Round Table and the Lady of the Lake it demonstrates the nature of the relationship between them. The qualities of Yin are dark, passive, slow, descending, female, cold and interior – a good description of the influence of the Lady of the Lake. Yang represents light, fire, sun, active, fast, hard, focused, ascending, male and aggressive – an apt description of the knights.
3   Probably by the novelist Edward Bulwer-Lytton in his novel of 1842, *Zanoni*.
4   The significance of the Garden of Eden with reference to the separation of the human and Faery races is discussed fully in *Red Tree, White Tree*.

CHAPTER SEVEN

The journey into Gorre: a Magical Ritual

T HIS CHAPTER PROVIDES YOU with a complete ritual of initiation into Faery. It is written for four participants who each mediate the role of one of the characters in the journey to Gorre that was described in the previous chapter. Each of these participants sits at one of the four quarters of the circle of the Temple, with an altar at the centre. You will find that it works best if you can perform it with at least three others, but it can be adapted for use with a partner, or you can work it on your own with a little extra effort. If you are working with a group, ideally the speaking roles should be taken by three men and one woman, but if this is not possible it is perfectly acceptable for a woman to mediate a man's part, or vice versa.

If you are working on your own, you can approach the central section of the ritual, which is a re-creation of the actual journey into the Kingdom of Gorre, in the same way as you have approached previous Inner journeys. Read it through several times until you are familiar with each stage and then follow it in your imagination. The opening section of the ritual, in which you invoke the presence of the four Inner beings who sit at the quarters of the Temple, will be a little more challenging! The best way to approach this is to turn and face each quarter in turn. Have the central altar between yourself and the quarter you are facing. Read each of the four invocations slowly, out loud, allowing yourself plenty of time to build the forms as described in the script. Have the four symbols ready on the altar before you start, so that instead of walking to the altar with each symbol, at the appropriate place in the ritual you can simply pick it up, slowly and solemnly raise it into the air, and then gently replace it.

If you are working with a partner, one of you should sit in the East and the other in the West. You can each mediate the Inner character in your quarter, but will have to visualise those in the North and South.

Remember that when you are working a magical ritual, and especially when you are entering the central section of the journey to the Inner location, you are not simply reading a story in an everyday state of consciousness. Magical ritual is performed in an enhanced state of consciousness and this is an opportunity to put all your previous work in increasing your awareness of Faery, and of the worlds they inhabit, into practice. Speak your words slowly, with a pause between each phrase, to allow the others to build the images as you describe them, and allow their meaning to come through. Much of the ritual's efficacy depends on how well you can build and hold the images in your mind's eye.

Collect the symbols you will need and arrange your Faery Temple, and the participants, as follows.

East	Gwenevere	A five-pointed star
South	Meleagant	A silver wand, tipped with red
West	Lancelot	A silver ring
North	Bademagus	A white crystal

Ideally, you should mark the Inner gateways at the four quarters of your Temple in some way, as this will indicate to those working with you from the Inner planes where these four quarter gateways are located. A candle placed at either side of each gateway is an ideal way of doing this. Ideally, each pair of candles should indicate the colours of the elements: white or yellow in the east to represent air, red in the south to represent fire, blue in the west to represent water and black in the north to represent earth. A candle should be placed on the central altar. You might also like to burn some delicate, rose-scented incense.

When the participants have taken their places, allow a few minutes for everyone to sink into a meditative state of consciousness. Then begin.

East   *Light the central candle, saying:*
A spark from the one true flame which shines through all the worlds.

Light a taper from the central candle and light all the quarter candles, starting in the East, saying:
In the name and power of the Angels of Air/Fire/Earth/Water, and of the One Deity who watches and protects human, Faery and creature, I open the East/South/West/North (*select the words appropriate to each quarter*)

Return to the East, extinguish your taper, and take your seat

East   The purpose of this ritual is to follow in the steps of Lancelot of the Lake, a knight of the Round Table who, following his heart's desire, discovered the hidden way into the Inner Mysteries of the Faery Kingdom of Gorre.
Four Innerworld beings sit at the quarters of this Temple. They hold and guard the gateways to the Inner worlds, and maintain the balanced flow of energy within the Temple. Let us sink into meditation and enter into the higher state of consciousness where we can begin to perceive the Inner beings who surround us...

PAUSE

In the East, I mediate the power and presence of Gwenevere, Queen of Faery. Let us visualise her presence, behind and above me. She is robed in palest green. She wears a tall crown of finest filigree gold. We are aware of the pale golden light which surrounds her, as of the dawn of a new day. It wafts into the Temple as if carried on a gentle wind fragranced with flowers and honey. This is the pure wind of the Paradise Garden. It uplifts the Temple with peace, and with love.
And let us also be aware of the greater figure who stands behind Gwenevere, that of Venus, the golden-eyed Goddess of love. She is so tall that she fills the Eastern quarter. Through her, flow the powers of compassion, harmony, and light. She reveals how heaven and earth may recognise each other, and be drawn together once more. We make contact with her through our hearts, knowing that she reveals the truth of our heart's desire.

I place this five-pointed star upon the altar, to indicate that the power and presence of Gwenevere, and of Venus, are working within this Faery Temple.

East slowly and deliberately places the star on the east side of the altar

South In the South, I mediate the power and presence of Meleagant, Prince of the Faery Kingdom of Gorre. Let us visualise his presence, behind and above me. He is a Faery warrior, wearing silver armour, emblazoned with red flame. He holds a silver spear. His energy is fierce, and his eyes burn with light. We are aware of his strong desire to protect the Faery kingdom of Gorre, and all the worlds and places of Faery, from the unthinking intrusions of the curious. He challenges any who attempt to enter his world without due care for the consequences.

And let us also be aware of the greater figure behind Meleagant, that of the Archangel Michael, whose spear of light descends from the perfection of the Heavenly worlds, through the surface of the earth, and into the deep places of the Faery kingdoms.

I place this wand upon the altar, to indicate that the power and presence of Meleagant, protector of Faery, and the Archangel Michael, are working within this Faery Temple.

South slowly places the wand upon the south side of the altar

West In the West, I mediate the power and presence of Lancelot of the Lake, knight of the Round Table. Let us visualise his presence, behind and above me. He is dressed in a white tunic, and carries a silver sword which shines with light. Lancelot was fostered by the Lady of the Lake, and he stands for all who have heard the call of Faery, guiding them through the many challenges upon the way.

It may be said that Lancelot carried his heart upon his sleeve, but his love for Gwenevere drove him to great feats of courage and endurance beyond that of personal desire. His ultimate quest is that of each one of us: to find and follow our heart's desire so that we may be led to spiritual truth.

And let us also be aware of the greater figure behind Lancelot, that of the Lady of the Lake in her aspect as the High Priestess of the Mysteries. She is seated upon a silver throne, surrounded by the still waters of a lake. Upon her lap is an open book. Upon her head is a silver crescent moon. Her eyes are calm, and filled with wisdom. She is far removed from our physical world but we may encounter her presence in the calm waters of the lake.

I place this silver ring upon the altar, to indicate that the power and presence of Lancelot of the Lake, who followed his heart's desire, and of the High Priestess of the Mysteries, are working within this Faery Temple.

West slowly places the silver ring on the west side of the altar

North In the North, I mediate the power and presence of Bademagus, Faery King of Gorre and High King of the Faeries. Let us visualise his presence, behind and above me. He is of great age. He is robed in emerald green. He has fine silver hair, upon which is set a slender band of gold, in which a single jewel sparkles with blue-white fire. His name indicates that he holds the status of Magus, which signifies that he has attained objective vision and knowledge of the Unseen worlds. He is of an earlier Age than his son Meleagant. His memory extends even to the times when the world had not yet taken on its present appearance but was still part of the star-lit world of the etheric plane. He oversees the struggles of Faery and humankind alike. He foresees the day, as yet in the remote future, when they will once again be as one.

And let us be aware also of the greater figure behind Bademagus, that of the Atlantean Merlin, Magician of the stellar realms. He raises one hand to us in greeting and acknowledgement.

I place this quartz crystal upon the altar, to indicate that the power and presence of Bademagus, King of the Faery Kingdom of Gorre and guardian of the Mysteries, and of Merlin, Magician of the stellar realms, are working within this Faery Temple.

North slowly places the quartz crystal on the north side of the altar

West Let us leave behind the things of the outer world, and in our imagination, take ourselves into the chamber of the Round Table ... where we take our seats. The pale violet veil hanging at the Western quarter begins to move slightly, as if blown by a gentle breath of wind. The veil dissolves, and as we sit at the Round Table we become aware that the Western quarter is now open to the influence of the Faery Kingdom of Gorre that lies beyond it. We hear the faint sound of tiny silver bells... We are aware that our inner senses are becoming refined, bringing a heightened awareness of the realities of the Inner planes. We perceive that the clear white light of Faery is entering our consciousness.

Let us listen to the story of Lancelot, who journeyed into the Faery Kingdom of Gorre, following where Gwenevere led him. Let us follow his story in our imagination and journey with him, building the images as they are described.

Lancelot was the son of King Ban of Benoic and Elaine. When he was still an infant, his parents were driven out from their kingdom, a misfortune so severe that it caused King Ban to die of a broken heart. But as they fled, the Lady of the Lake, who had foreseen these events, appeared to them and took the infant Lancelot into her arms. She carried him away, and brought him up as her own child, in her own country. Some called her country the Island of Maidens, and described it as a beautiful place of perpetual Spring. Others know of it as the island of Avalon, hidden beneath the mists which gather over the lake.

East In the Island of Maidens, Lancelot learnt much of the nature of Faeries and of their origins, although he was taught little of the knight's skills of fighting and jousting. When he reached the age of fifteen, he left his foster mother and returned to the human world, making his way to King Arthur's court. He was accepted as a knight of the Round Table and, together with his companions, he encountered many adventures which tested him in the ways of the world. Immersed in the world, he began to forget his Faery upbringing.

But in time, the ways of world brought him low in spirit, and so he left the court of the Round Table, and wandered alone in the wildness of nature, seeking solace. Eventually, after many months, he came to the windswept cliffs of Tintagel, the place where King Arthur himself had been born, and where much that is new, still comes into being.

West   Here, the Lady of the Lake appeared to him again. She cared for him until he was healed of his sadness. And then she told him that he was to return to King Arthur's court and undertake a great task that would be revealed to him. And so Lancelot returned to his companions of the Round Table.

South   When he arrived at the court, he found King Arthur sitting at the Round Table, with his knights. But there came in to where they sat an armed knight, girded with a sword, and bareheaded. He strode across the room, clasping the hilt of his sword with his right hand in a show of confidence, and said: "I am Meleagant, son of King Bademagus of Gorre. In that land, King Arthur, many of your people are held prisoner, yet none of your knights dares cross the bridge into Gorre and rescue them."

And having so said, he turned on his heel, and strode out into the great forest that lies between the worlds.

East   He was followed by Queen Gwenevere, who also departed from the court of the Round Table. She went with Meleagant, travelling with him through the great forest, towards the Faery Kingdom of Gorre.

Meleagant and Gwenevere rise. Together, they walk slowly, clockwise, once around the Temple and then resume their seats

North   Let us follow Meleagant and Gwenevere in our imagination, as they enter the forest between the worlds.

Imagine that you are standing in a clearing in the forest. It is so quiet that you can hear a leaf fall. Ancient oaks grow all about you, taller than any you have seen. They form a green canopy high above your head, through which the dappled sunlight streams down onto the ferns and mosses that cover the forest floor. These trees, and ferns, are many thousands of years old. You stand, and watch, and wait, in the silence. Time stands still.

East   You become aware of the vibrant green energy of the forest, an energy so strong that it begins to manifest as a green light which plays and dances about you. You become aware of the Faeries of the forest, watching as they gradually take form within the green light: immortal Beings as old as the forest itself.

And now, in the distance, you see Gwenevere and Meleagant, walking towards you along a grassy path. Meleagant is dressed in shining silver armour, and leading a white horse. Gwenevere is dressed in palest green. She is in her element, at one with the trees and the green light, joyous in her freedom. For a moment, you believe that they are coming to meet you, but they turn off the path and into the trees. Soon they are lost to sight. Yet you know that they were aware of your presence, and they seemed to invite you to follow them.

South Distant sounds break the silence. You hear swords clashing, metal upon metal, and cries and shouts. And now you see many figures running through the trees. You see Lancelot, and other knights, fighting in noise and confusion. They continue to fight, running and shouting, but eventually disappear in the direction taken by Gwenevere and Meleagant. The sounds fade. Silence returns.

You decide to follow them, and take the path into the trees…

The air grows cooler, and the trees on either side crowd in upon you, blocking out much of the light. The path leads you deep into the forest. The light grows dim. There is no sign of the knights, or of Meleagant and Gwenevere. You are anxious to find some shelter before night falls.

West Ahead of you, you see an ancient hall built of stone. Its walls are dark, and its few windows are small and narrow. It does not look welcoming, although its imposing wooden door is ajar. Slowly, and with care, you push open the door and walk in. You enter a great hall.

North At the far end of the hall, on a low altar, a candle has been lit as if in expectation of your arrival. An odour of incense hangs upon the air. Two maidens, one robed in red, the other in white, kneel in prayer at either side of the altar. They do not look up at your approach. Between you and the altar are three narrow couches. Two are covered in white linen cloth and the third, in the centre, and higher than the other two, is covered with yellow velvet. You realise that they have been prepared for your coming. You understand that you will not be able to continue your journey into Gorre unless you are able to meet the tests which you will encounter here. If you do not feel ready, you may return to your own place and time with impunity. The hall will still be here when you are ready to return...

East If you decide to continue, you lie down upon the couch and, affirming your desire to experience and confront all that is necessary in order to enter the Kingdom of Gorre, you prepare yourself for what may befall.

You gaze upwards towards the roof. You find that you are looking up into the night sky. There are no stars, only a deep velvet darkness. You lie motionless, allowing the vision of the dome of the star-filled sky to fill your consciousness...

After a while, you see a single point of white light, infinitely high in the sky. The point of light grows in size and intensity. You realise that it is travelling directly towards you. And as it travels, you see that it throws out white sparks of light, like shooting stars. Some of these white sparks gather together as if in a celestial dance, and form star-clusters, and spirals, and galaxies.

South The single spark of light continues to move towards you. But now it burns red. Still it sends out sparks of light, and some of these red sparks gather together, and begin to form orbs of light.

West And you see now that a pathway of light is opening up, a celestial spear of light, in the night sky. It continues to descend until it pauses momentarily, suspended above the altar. The altar is set ablaze with light, in which red and white sparks of fire are intermingled. The entire hall is filled with its light.

North The spear of light continues to descend. It passes through the altar, and down into the earth beneath. The flames subside. The burning lights grow dim. The hall returns to its former state, lit only by the single flickering candle on the altar.

East You rise to your feet, a little shaken by this experience, but transformed in spirit. You see that the two maidens at the altar are now also standing. They smile in recognition of what you have witnessed. Many Seekers have come this far, but have seen nothing except the four stone walls. You would like to ask them more, but realise that the vision you have seen is one to treasure; it is for you alone to interpret. The two maidens indicate that you should now leave the hall, and gesture towards a heavy curtain in the wall behind the altar.

North   You move towards it. The maidens pull aside the curtain, and to your surprise, bright sunlight greets you. You step outside, and walk into the comforting warmth of a summer's day.

West   The forest has disappeared. A meadow of flowers stretches out before you, bright in the summer sunshine. Refreshed and with lifted spirits, you continue on your way.

A river lies in the distance. On the path which runs alongside it, you see a procession of knights and ladies, some riding upon white horses, some walking. Faint sounds of music and laughter float towards you on the air. The procession is led by Gwenevere and Meleagant. You would like to run to catch up with them, but realise that your efforts would be in vain: you cannot hope to reach them, but can only observe which way they go, and follow their path. You start to make your way towards the river, and they are soon gone from your sight.

East   Suddenly, in the meadow, you come across a well. You stop to look at it. It is surrounded by a low, stone parapet. Lying on the parapet is a silver comb. A single golden hair is held within the comb. You know that it is Gwenevere's. You do not touch it, but sit down on the stone parapet. You peer over, and look down into the well.

It is filled with starlight.

You take time to reflect on this puzzle…

PAUSE

You must continue your journey.

The Kingdom of Gorre is not far away. But in order to reach it, you must now choose one of three ways that present themselves to you.

North   To your left lies the Stone Passage. It is formed by a double row of ancient standing stones, leading to a stone circle. To walk this way is to tread the path of the Laws of the Universe. This path leads to the knowledge and understanding of the universal laws of creation. Each stone, in itself, and in its relation to the others, represents the cycles and periodicity of the forces that govern the universe and all created life within the universe. The worlds of human and Faery alike are governed by these laws. These ancient granite stones, quarried from the earth but sparkling with crystals of star-fire, hold the patterns and traces of universal memory.

But there are also dangers on this path. The Stone Passage is a narrow path, and can all too easily close in on the Seeker, shutting out the light of the world. This is the path of the intellect, which believes it can unravel the secrets of existence through its own power alone. Unless this path is trodden with the heart and soul, as well as the head, it will lead only to sterility.

South   To your right lies an attractive path through the flowers and grasses. This path leads to the Underwater Bridge. It will lead you into Gorre by a way which lies beneath the deep river that borders Gorre on all sides. This is the path of experience of the Forces of Nature. To take this path is to learn, through direct engagement with the elemental forces, of the driving powers which infuse the natural world. Here can be found the great Elemental Beings, and the Angelic powers which lie behind them. This path takes you beneath the appearance of the material world to the powers which lie beneath, the same powers that are also found deep within the human psyche. This is the path of inspiration, and of attraction and desire.

There are dangers, too, on this path. The Underwater Bridge cannot be seen in the clear light of day. Only its reflection can be seen on the surface of the water. The path towards this bridge is easy, but it is not an easy bridge to cross. Once you step on it, you will find it difficult to distinguish between above and below. This is the path of the creative forces, but unless you use your head, as well as following your heart, this path may lead you only into deep water.

West   You consider, and reject, the paths to the left and right. And when you have made your decision to keep on the straight and narrow path that leads directly on, you see in front of you the Sword Bridge that crosses over the river into the kingdom of Gorre. The bridge is very narrow, and very long, and gleams with white light. This is the Path of the Spirit. If you take this path into Faery, you will do so with a clear awareness of your own Individuality, neither swayed by the glamour and illusion of the Faery worlds nor, on the other hand, believing that you can reach the Faery realm simply through book learning and knowledge. But do not assume that you know all there is to discover about the Faery kingdoms. On the other side of the bridge you may not find what you expect.

East   You can only move forward in faith. You place one foot on the bridge and pause to find your balance. You realise that any disturbance or imbalance within you will cause you to sway either one way or the other and lose your footing. You step from the land onto the bridge ... and move forward slowly, step by step. Gradually, you make your way across the bridge. If you keep steady in spirit, and steady and controlled in your emotions, you will keep steady in body.

And as you walk, step by step, you find that the weight of your worldly cares falls from you. The sacrifice and suffering of the physical world, and your bodily cares, slip from your shoulders. You had forgotten what it felt like to be free of the burdens of the world. You are becoming a body of light. Your aura is filled with colour and beauty, and shines with light. You move forward with more confidence, each step becoming easier, and more joyful. And with each step you take, the light about you shines more brightly.

You reach firm land. But you have not arrived in the Faery Kingdom that you expected. All signs of human and Faery life have entirely disappeared. You have entered a land, and a time, far beyond Faery. You see two tall pillars ahead of you, shining out through the mist. You realise that the two pillars are trees, but of an immense height, and of a wondrous beauty such as you have never seen on earth. The tree to your right is silver, and the tree to your left is gold.

The tree to your right is the Faery Tree, the Tree of Immortality. It is a living fountain of light. It is translucent, shining silvery-white. It has no fixed form, but is a shimmering stream of energy. It has no leaves, but is formed of a thousand delicate fronds and tendrils which unfurl from its trunk in glorious abundance.

You realise that tree extends as far beneath the ground as it does above. It is fed by four deep roots, which also are shining white and reach far into the earth, as if to the four quarters of the world; a network of veins and arteries which carry and support the etheric life-blood of the earth.

The rhythm of this tree is quick, and pulsating; its energy is sparkling, flickering and dancing. Its tendrils soar towards the sky, as if to try to touch the stars, and indeed it seems as if the stars themselves reach down to kindle the tree with their inimitable light. The tips of the tree's delicate fronds glitter with star-dust.

The Faery Tree of Immortality has no fruits or flowers. But when you look closely within its ethereal branches, you see tiny gemstones of liquid light flowing within, both up and down the tree, as if swept along on an invisible tide of light. The Faery Tree contains within itself an endless cycle of renewal whereby the glittering stars above, seeking the earth, flow down through the tree into the ground, where they crystallise into gemstones. And the gemstones within the deep earth, seeking the stars, dissolve into liquid light and flow up through the tree to rejoin their companions in the stars.

West The tree to your left is the Tree of Humanity, the Tree of Knowledge. It, too, is unlike the trees you would find in a forest, although it bears a closer resemblance to them than the Faery Tree. The Tree of Humanity is radiant gold in colour. It manifests every shade of gold, from deep red-gold, through bronze and amber, to the palest of golden hints. Its twigs and branches are covered in tiny leaves of great beauty and perfection. They are of a multitude of shapes and sizes.

The Tree of Humanity also bears many flowers that come and go like bursts of flame, so that the tree is lit with a constant display of ephemeral fires. These flames have brief lives, and each soon coalesces into a golden sphere, like a red-gold apple. When you turn your attention to any one of these fruits, you see that its light soon begins to dim. As its light fades, it detaches from the tree, falling gently and silently onto the earth below. The earth enfolds it, receiving it as its own.

Gwenevere rises, and stands to the East of the altar

North You see now that Gwenevere is standing beneath the Faery Tree of Immortality. And you realise how closely her life-energy is connected with the rhythm and quality of the Faery Tree, as if they were one.

Lancelot rises, and stands to the West of the altar

South   You see that Lancelot is standing beneath the Tree of Humanity. And you realise how closely his life-energy is connected with the rhythm and quality of this Tree of Knowledge, as if they were one.

North   They each move slowly towards the other, and as they do so, they seem to bring with them the energies of the two trees, as if they were each a living extension of the tree's aura. Gwenevere of the silver Tree of Immortality, and Lancelot of the golden Tree of Knowledge.

Lancelot and Gwenevere each slowly raise their arms above the altar

South   As they meet, they slowly raise their arms high towards each other. And between them, a twin spiral of energy begins to form. One spiral is of the silvery-white flowing energy of the Faery Tree, and the other of the mixed golden hues of the Tree of Humanity.

North   And you see that this twin spiral of energies is expanding, growing taller and wider, and that it now encompasses both Gwenevere and Lancelot.

South   It continues to expand until each of the trees is caught up in the swirling spiral of energy, so that the silver lights of the Faery Tree are swirling amongst the golden leaves of the Tree of Humanity.

North   And the golden bursts of light, and the golden apples, and the falling fruits, have been taken up within the silver fountain of the Faery Tree.

South   Let us watch how this twin spiral grows and develops…

Lancelot and Gwenevere continue to hold their position until they intuit that the vision is coming to a close. They slowly lower their arms, and return to their seats.

East   *Raises right hand.* With the power of Venus mediated through the Eastern quarter, I bless this vision of the conjoined Trees of Faery and Humanity, that they may continue to work for the evolution of all who inhabit the earth.

South   *Raises right hand.* With the power of the Archangel Michael mediated through the Southern quarter, I bless this vision of the conjoined Trees of Faery and Humanity, that they may continue to work for the evolution of all who inhabit the earth.

West *Raises right hand.* With the power of the Lady of the Lake, High Priestess of these Mysteries mediated through the Western quarter, I bless this vision of the conjoined Trees of Faery and Humanity, that they may continue to work for the evolution of all who inhabit the earth.

North *Raises right hand.* With the power of Merlin of Atlantis mediated through the Northern quarter, I bless this vision of the conjoined Trees of Faery and Humanity, that they may continue to work for the evolution of all who inhabit the earth.

East Our work is concluded. We see the pale violet veil fall back over the gateway to the Western quarter of the chamber of the Round Table. It is time for us to return to our own place and time. Let us each slowly return to our normal waking consciousness. But let us think on these things, and continue to mediate our realisations and understanding through our everyday lives.

*When all have returned to the present, **East** stands, turns to the East, (then moves to South, West and North) and says:*
In the name and power of the Angels of Air/Fire/Earth/Water, and the One God who watches and protects human, Faery and creature, I give thanks for your presence and close the East/South/West/Northern quarter. *East extinguishes the quarter candles.*

Finally, East extinguishes the central candle.

All leave the Faery Temple when they are ready.

CHAPTER EIGHT

The Faery Kingdom of Lyonesse

THE NEXT FAERY KINGDOM we shall explore is Lyonesse, the Kingdom of Gwenevere's father Leodegrance, and the place of her childhood. The gateway into Lyonesse is found in the eastern quarter of the chamber of the Round Table.

The nature of the magical work of the Round Table that you will experience in Lyonesse represents a distinct step up from the work of Sorelois and Gorre, and in Lyonesse you will begin to access the levels of consciousness that are related to the stars. Lyonesse forms the gateway to the stellar worlds that are the Faeries' spiritual home, and the wisdom of the stars constitutes a significant part of the more advanced symbolism of the Round Table. As we explored in Chapter Two, Merlin passed the guardianship of the Round Table to Leodegrance after Uther PenDragon had died, and with good reason. Although Leodegrance appears only briefly in the legends, both he and his Faery kingdom contain a depth of meaning which fully repays further investigation.

The challenge of the Kingdom of Lyonesse is very practical, although hardly down to earth! It is that you familiarise yourself with a group of twelve constellations in the northern hemisphere that is specifically linked to the Round Table. All the information you will need in order to learn about these constellations, first in theory, and then in practice as you begin to explore them in your imagination, will be found in the following pages. But before you make a start, here are the magical correspondences of Lyonesse for you to keep in mind.

MAGICAL CORRESPONDENCES OF THE KINGDOM OF LYONESSE	
Direction:	**East**
Symbol:	**A quartz crystal cluster**
Challenge:	**To learn the star-lore of the Round Table**
Gift:	**Finding the gateway to the stars**
Initiators:	**Gwenevere, King Leodegrance**

Stars and star-groups are part of the spiritual influence on Faeries and humans alike, and to reach up into the stars and make contact with their energy is to discover a shared source of creative vitality and spiritual impulse. In your journey towards the Faeries and their world you may find that an Inner veil impedes your progress until you are able to enter the stellar levels in your consciousness, and this level of Inner awareness is essential to a full understanding of the symbolism of the Round Table.

Our relationship with the stars is a living progression, not a fixed science, and it has developed and changed over the centuries according to the needs of the epoch. The ways in which the astronomers of ancient civilisations understood the stars and interpreted their meaning is not necessarily appropriate for us now. Once you have begun to forge your own personal connection with the constellations of the night sky you will find that a gateway begins to form within your consciousness, a channel of communication begins to open, energy is exchanged, and the presences of the stellar worlds will begin to make themselves known to you. In making this connection for yourself, you will not only be opening up new areas of your own awareness of the universe but you will be contributing to a relationship with the stellar worlds that ultimately has relevance for all humanity.

Although the Faeries have continued to maintain a lively relationship with the stars, over the last 2000 years or so humankind has increasingly focused on the single star we call the Sun. If we were to develop a fraction of the awareness we have of the Sun, in relation to just a few of the other stars, imagine what an effect this would have on our lives! But the great civilisations of ancient times such as the Babylonians, Chinese, Persians and Egyptians were acutely aware of the stars, and there is much evidence to suggest that the ancient

Britons still practiced this art. They had precise knowledge of the stars' location in the skies, of their relative movement, and of their qualities and attributions. Their relationship with the stars was alive and dynamic; they used them for navigational purposes, they oriented their Temples on them and they knew that the lives of their heroes and heroines were dynamically reflected in the night sky. Above all, their awareness of humanity's continuing relationship with the stars after death was well developed; it formed an important part of their belief and was of especial importance in the magical work of their Priesthood.

Most ancient civilisations developed their own systems for identifying and naming the stars and organising them into groups. Only a few groups of stars are so distinct that they have been universally recognized, such as Orion's belt, the Pleiades and the Great Bear or Plough. A list of 48 anciently recognized constellations appeared in a book written around AD150 by the Greco-Egyptian astronomer Claudius Ptolemy. In the 15th century, sailors venturing south of the equator discovered many new stars that were not in Ptolemy's list, and added new constellations as they perceived them. Later still, when much larger telescopes were invented, astronomers added a few more groups that had not attracted earlier attention because they contain no bright stars, and there are now 88 generally recognised constellations. But it seems very likely that groups of stars have been identified as long as there have been humans and Faeries to look at them. The cave paintings in Lascaux in France feature several recognisable constellations, and these paintings are at least 17,000 years old.

Today, however, although most people can probably name the twelve 'Sun signs' (the constellations across which the Sun travels in the course of a year) and perhaps have an idea of the characteristics of their own birth sign, not many of us can identify more than a few actual stars or constellations in the sky. This is not simply a matter of lack of interest: the increasing light pollution that afflicts our world can make it very difficult to see any but the brightest constellations, and the breathtaking sight of the glittering stars in an unpolluted night sky which was once our birthright is now a rare vision. But light pollution is not the only reason for our neglect of this part of our spiritual heritage. The stars have not only receded in our skies but also in our consciousness, and many people have given up on them altogether.

Although it can be more difficult to see the night skies now than it was even fifty years ago, you will find, with a little perseverance, that you can see a lot more than you might have thought. If you make the most of the opportunities available to you, and if you have prepared yourself for each opportunity by studying the shape and position of the constellations on a star-map beforehand so that you know exactly what you are looking for, you will gain immense satisfaction from being able to identify more than you imagined possible when you look into the night sky. If you are driving back to the city at night, stop the car in a lay-by and look up at the stars. If you visit a friend in the country, or have a holiday by the sea, take every chance you can to look at the stars. It is not necessary to own a telescope, but a pair of binoculars will make a huge difference to the number of stars you can see. If you can share the opportunity with a friend, even better. Most people are delighted when the bright stars and constellations are pointed out to them and a little knowledge of the sky above our heads helps everyone to make sense of their place in the universe.

As preparation for the practical work which comes later in this chapter you will need to absorb a certain amount of information about the stars. However, learning about them is not just an intellectual exercise. As you learn the shape and position of each constellation and hold this knowledge in your awareness, so you will be opening to its qualities and influences even if you have not yet seen the constellation in the sky. It's rather like pressing a light switch. The names of the stars are a useful tool, as is a map of their location, but you will begin to find when you have opened your consciousness to their appearance and characteristics by learning about them in theory, that you are also connecting up with them in your imagination. This will also have the effect of opening a gateway in your relationship with the Faeries just as if you were learning to speak their language. Our mutual inheritance lies in the stars, and by reaching back to them we can reach back to our shared origins.

THE ROUND TABLE OF THE STARS

In recent years, the Round Table has attracted interest as a representation of the Solar zodiac that can be seen set out in the actual landscape, most notably around Glastonbury. The explanation of the Round Table as an image of the zodiac would seem to make very good sense. The twelve-fold division of the year forms the background to most modern civilisations, so there would appear to be every good reason that a symbolic representation of this pattern should be demonstrated in the Round Table. There are many twelve-fold systems which resonate with this pattern, such as Christ and the twelve disciples, or Hercules and his twelve labours. In like fashion, the Round Table is often described as seating King Arthur and his twelve bravest knights, although there is no general agreement as to who these twelve knights might be. Lancelot, Kay and Gawain are perhaps the most frequently mentioned, although in fact well over a hundred knights are named throughout the legends.

But there is a fundamental problem in identifying the Round Table with the zodiac, which is that the zodiac is a twelve-fold *solar* based system. Gwenevere is a Faery, as is her father Leodegrance, and the Sun does not have the overriding importance to the Faeries as it does to humans; it does not form the centre of their universe and dominate their life-energy to the exclusion of the other stars as it does for humankind. The Faeries' lives are not ruled by the twelve-fold division of the year into the Sun signs and this pattern is of little relevance to them. For these reasons alone, it is unlikely that Merlin would have passed a representation of the solar zodiac into their keeping, nor would there have been much sense in Gwenevere conveying a solar-based system of wisdom as a marriage gift to the human King Arthur. He had as little need of such information as Gwenevere and her Faery father had the ability to offer it. And yet the concept of the Round Table as a mirror of the heavens is impossible to ignore. A magical, circular symbol must surely refer somehow to the dome of the skies, but if it does not refer to the solar zodiac then to which stars, or pattern of stars, does it refer?

The next most distinctive group of stars in the northern hemisphere is the group of five constellations known collectively as the circumpolar stars, and consists of the Great Bear, the Little Bear, Draco the dragon, Cepheus the King and Cassiopeia the Queen. This group of constellations appears to turn anticlockwise around the north celestial pole once every twenty four hours, and is therefore sometimes referred to as a wheel, or likened to a mill-wheel turning about the polar axis. These constellations were especially important to the spiritual beliefs of the ancient Egyptians who gave them the evocative title of the Imperishable Stars because, to observers from mid-northern latitudes, they do not ever sink below the horizon.[1]

These five constellations do indeed lie at the heart of Arthurian mythology. The sinuous form of Draco, especially the three stars which form the head of the dragon or 'Pen Dragon', together with the Great and Little Bears, form the starry background to the Age of Arthur's father Uther PenDragon that witnessed the preparation for Arthur's coming. The connection between the constellation of Draco and Uther as head of the PenDragon Dynasty is explored fully in *Red Tree, White Tree*.[2] But by the time Gwenevere entered the mythology, this part of the story had already long taken place and its events worked through, so it would have made little sense for her to have brought with her, into the human world, a representation of what had already been achieved. The gift she brought from Faery must surely have been something that offered a symbolic representation of Faery magic such that it would become a template for future work, rather than represent the past. As we have seen in Chapter Two, Merlin makes it abundantly clear that the magical Order of the Round Table he introduced into Arthur's court contained new, and different, levels of meaning to that which had gone before.

If we focus on the idea that the purpose of Gwenevere's marriage to King Arthur was to initiate a reunion between Faery and human and to provide the environment in which this might be explored magically, it seems likely that the circle of stars or constellations that form the Round Table in the stars will reflect and symbolise this purpose. The circle is unlikely to be the twelve constellations of the solar zodiac which are so closely related to human activity, nor the five constellations of the circumpolar stars which are linked to King Arthur's predecessors, but a third circle that lies between them, touching them both but separate to them. We might expect it to contain groups of stars that are particularly relevant to humanity *and* those that are especially connected with Faery, so that it forms a talismanic symbol of the relationship between them, referring to their history and also acting as a demonstration of the way forward to a new resolution. It will incorporate all the work of the Round Table that is represented by the five Faery kingdoms, but on a higher level.

In fact a ring of constellations which lies between the circles of the solar zodiac and the circumpolar stars does emerge very clearly. It is highlighted on the star-map: the Round Table of the Stars. The five circumpolar constellations lie at its centre, and the circle of the solar zodiac touches it at a tangent. Twelve constellations are positioned either on or immediately either side of its circumference: Cancer, Leo and Coma Berenice; Boötes, Corona Borealis and Hercules; Lyra and Cygnus; Andromeda, Perseus and Auriga; and Gemini. The Milky Way also plays a significant role in the Round Table of the Stars, as we shall explore later.

Each of these constellations will be described in detail in the following pages, but for the moment we shall focus on the three constellations that are specifically connected with the Kingdom of Lyonesse. First, the constellation that represents Gwenevere herself, which is the triangle of stars that forms Coma Berenice or Berenice's Hair. As you look at the stellar Round Table, this constellation lies nearest to you and points the way clockwise about its circumference like an arrow.

On Gwenevere's other side is the group of stars that represent her father Leodegrance, the constellation of Leo the Lion. He is looking towards his watery Kingdom of Lyonesse which is represented by the constellation of Cancer. Gwenevere and Leodegrance teach the knowledge and wisdom of the stars, and Lyonesse itself forms the gateway through which the stellar Round Table can be accessed.

CREATING YOUR BOOK OF STARS

As you work through the next chapters and explore the constellations of the Round Table, you will probably find it helpful to make a drawing of each group of stars as you learn about it, and the best way of doing this is to create your own Book of Stars for this very purpose. Some sheets of blank paper and a pencil are all that you need. You may already have some familiarity with the night sky, or perhaps on the other hand you can only name and recognise one or two of the most famous constellations such as Orion and the Great Bear. But for the present purpose it is by no means a disadvantage if you have no previous knowledge of the stars because it is your own, personal response to them and your own realisation of their qualities and symbolism which are important. Time spent in studying the star-map

NORTHERN HEMISPHERE

THE ROUND TABLE OF THE STARS

and learning the shapes and relative positions of the constellations of the Round Table will not be wasted.

You might also like to buy some tiny, imitation gemstones such as are used in costume jewellery. These need not cost you much but if you lay them out on your talismanic Round Table in the shape of the constellation you are working with you will find that they form a very effective symbol. These sparkling shapes will also attract the attention of the Faeries, who love such things.

The manner in which the constellations have been named and identified through the ages is still very much a mystery. Humanity's relationship with the stars is complex, and different civilisations have interpreted them each in their own way. Sometimes it has happened that astronomers from different parts of the world have agreed on the shape of a particular constellation and have come to the same conclusion as to its qualities, but equally they have often reached widely differing interpretations. Behind this puzzle lies an even greater mystery, which is that most of the constellations tend to look nothing like their namesakes!

The best time to start to identify the stars and constellations is this very night, unless the sky is completely clouded over. If it is, you will have to restrict yourself to studying the star-map. When you first begin to look at the stars, remember is that it takes ten minutes or so for your eyes to adjust fully to the darkness, so allow yourself enough time to make this adjustment. The easiest constellation to locate, because it is one of the brightest and most distinctively shaped, and as one of the circumpolar constellations it is always visible in the northern hemisphere, is the **Great Bear**, also known as the Plough, Arthur's Chariot and the Big Dipper. Although this last name is the least evocative of its titles it is very useful for when you are using this constellation as a guide to finding the other star-groups, because you can readily distinguish the curved handle of the 'dipper' from its rectangular 'bowl.' Not only is the Great Bear or Dipper one of the easiest constellations to identify but it also acts as a pointer from which almost all the other constellations of the Round Table can be located. The Great Bear is frequently associated with King Arthur and it therefore makes perfect sense that it should function as the directing power of the Round Table!

Once you have located the Great Bear in the night skies, make your contact with the seven bright stars of this constellation. Using the same technique of softening your gaze that you use when adjusting your vision and consciousness to that of the Faeries about you, be receptive to these stars. Give yourself plenty of time to discover this new skill, and keep an open mind as to what this and other constellations may reveal to you. Approach each star-gazing session as a meditation, and record your experiences and realisations in your Book of Stars. You will soon find that your sense of the stellar worlds is beginning to open up, as if you are using muscles that have been neglected for some time.

When you have spent time in contemplation of the constellation as a whole, focus on the last two stars of the 'bowl' of the Dipper. These stars are called Merak and Dubhe. If you draw an imaginary line between them, and then extend this line for about five times that distance, you will arrive at Polaris, the Pole star of the present age. Polaris is by no means the brightest star in the sky but it is always visible in reasonable conditions and it is always located due north. This makes it an important star for you to locate as you begin to navigate your way about the stellar Round Table. The Pole star is actually the last star in the tail of the **Little Bear**, another of the circumpolar constellations, whose shape oddly mirrors that of the Great Bear. It is fainter than the Great Bear, but you might be able to pick it out once you have found the Pole Star.

Unlike the circumpolar constellations, the twelve constellations of the Round Table are not always visible throughout the year, so you will need to know which ones to look for in each season unless you are able to star-gaze at all hours of the night. The three constellations that are the stellar representations of the Kingdom of Lyonesse – Cancer, Leo and Coma Berenice – are best seen in the Spring evenings soon after it has got dark.

You can easily locate **Leo** from The Great Bear. Extend an imaginary line again, but this time in the opposite direction of the Pole star and from the first two stars of the bowl of the dipper. If you continue the line for about six times the distance between them, you will arrive at Regulus, a brilliant pale blue star at the heart of the constellation of Leo. Regulus is sometimes described as the last star of a back-to-front question mark, which might also help you locate the constellation. The tip of Leo's tail is marked by the bright star Denebola. If you have learnt and remembered the pattern of the stars of this constellation before you search for it in the sky, you may be able to pick out the stars which lie between these two bright luminaries, and which form the body of Leo.

To locate the constellation of **Cancer**, draw an imaginary line from Denebola to Regulus, and extend it almost exactly the same distance again. This will take you to the middle of Cancer. It is not a bright constellation, but if you have memorised its shape, and try to locate it on a dark clear night, you may be able to find it. The beginning of March is probably the best time to view it.

The constellation which represents Gwenevere herself in her starry form is **Coma Berenice**. Coma Berenice is a most beautiful star cluster but it is elusive to locate and you are unlikely to see it easily without binoculars. It shines with a unique, delicate twinkling, but although it enchanted the star-gazers of ancient times it is now nearly lost to us because of light pollution. How apt a constellation to represent Gwenevere! Coma Berenice can also be located from the Great Bear. Draw an imaginary line from the first star of the curve of the 'handle' to Denebola, the bright star in the tail of Leo. You will skirt the edge of Coma Berenice which lies about two-thirds of the way along that line. Alternatively, if you have already located the constellation of Boötes, Coma Berenice lies half-way between Boötes and Leo. Study your star map and you may find your own ways of locating Gwenevere amongst the stars. If you succeed, you will feel as if you have discovered a lost treasure, but don't be discouraged if it remains beyond your sight. Later in this chapter you will visit it in your imagination which is almost as good, if not better.

These are the Spring constellations, so if you are beginning your work with this chapter at another time of year you will need to begin your exploration of the stellar Round Table according to the season. We shall explore all the constellations in turn, travelling in a clockwise journey about the Round Table. On the map of the stellar Round Table, if you follow the direction of Gwenevere's arrow, the first constellation you will arrive at is that of **Boötes** the Herdsman. The constellation's brightest star Arcturus sits exactly on the table's circumference. You can locate Arcturus from the Great Bear by continuing the curve of the handle a long way down through the sky until you come to a distinctive bright red-orange star: this is Arcturus. The star lies at the base of a vast kite-shape formed by the five brightest stars in the constellation of Boötes. You might be surprised at how much sky this figure covers. In late Spring evenings this constellation will be high in the sky.

Once you have located the kite shape of Boötes, you can easily pick out the next constellation in the Round Table, **Corona Borealis** or the Crown of the North Wind, with its very distinctive 'bowl' of seven stars.

Beyond the Crown of the North Wind lies the fainter constellation of **Hercules** which is best seen in late Spring and early Summer. This constellation is more difficult to locate, but if you have learnt the pattern of its stars from the map before you try to find it in the sky, and have successfully found the Crown of the North Wind, you will find Hercules.

If you are star-gazing in Summer, as an alternative to orienting yourself from the Great Bear, you might like to focus on the distinctive 'Summer Triangle' of stars which will be almost overhead in the late evenings of the summer months. This triangle is formed by the brilliant blue-white star Vega in the constellation of **Lyra**, the star Deneb in the constellation of **Cygnus** the Swan which flies along the Milky Way (both of these constellations are part of the stellar Round Table) and the star Altair in the constellation of **Aquila** the Eagle.

If you have located Lyra by finding its brightest star Vega, you can locate Corona Borealis and Boötes by drawing an imaginary line between the two stars Vega and Arcturus. The line will pass through Hercules and skirt the edge of Corona Borealis and Boötes before it arrives at Arcturus.

With Cygnus, we arrive at the starry river of the Milky Way which forms a distinct boundary across the Round Table. The constellations that lie on the other side have a very different feel to them, as you will discover when you explore them later. The constellations of the Round Table that lie on the far side of the Milky Way are Andromeda, Perseus and Auriga the Charioteer.

If you are beginning your study of the stars in Autumn, the distinctive 'W' shape of **Cassiopeia** the Queen, one of the circumpolar constellations, will be nearly overhead in the evening. It is one of the easier constellations to pick out, but if you can't locate it immediately, return to the Great Bear and draw another imaginary line, this time from the second star of the curve or 'handle' up through the Pole star, and you will arrive at Cassiopeia. If you study the star map, you will see how Cassiopeia forms a pointer to **Andromeda** and **Perseus**. Andromeda in particular is not very easy to identify but if you learn the shape before you look for her in the sky you should find her without too much difficulty.

This just leaves Auriga and Gemini, which are best seen in late Autumn and Winter evenings. The constellation of **Auriga** contains only five stars in an approximate pentagram shape, but it contains the sixth brightest star in the sky, Capella. You can locate Capella from the Great Bear by drawing yet another imaginary line, this time across the two top stars in the 'bowl.' Capella is approximately five times the distance between them. If you have learnt the pentagram shape of the constellation of Auriga in relation to Capella you should be able to identify it in the sky without much difficulty.

The final constellation of the stellar Round Table is **Gemini**. The twin bright stars of Gemini can also easily be found from the Great Bear. If you study the star map you will soon see the relationship between them: they are separated from the Great Bear by a large area of sky in which there are very few bright stars. Or, you can start from the star which joins the end of the handle to the bowl or dipper. (It is the fourth of the seven stars in whichever direction you count them.) Extend a line from this star to the lower of the two 'pointer' stars and continue until you reach the bright star Pollux. Its twin star Castor is nearby. But if you can see the Great Bear, you can easily find both Auriga and Gemini by crossing over the area of dark sky until you reach the next bright stars.

These are the simple principles of star-navigation for the constellations of the Round Table. Once you have learnt them you will soon find your way around the skies. Whenever you can, try to locate some of these constellations according to the season. Autumn is often the best time for star-gazing because the atmospheric conditions can be good and clear and you don't have to wait up too long before nightfall!

With each of these constellations, make sure that you have memorised its shape so that you can build it in your mind's eye, and this will make your star-gazing opportunities much easier. A good way to do this is simply to study the pattern of its stars and then try to draw the shape from memory. This is a useful meditation exercise in itself because when you hold the constellation in your thoughts and imagination you are already beginning to build a dynamic relationship with it.

LYONESSE, FAERY KINGDOM OF THE STARS

Having learnt some of background and theory of the starry Round Table you are ready to begin to journey into it in your imagination, and the Faery Kingdom of Lyonesse forms the gateway. As preparation for the journey into Lyonesse you will need to be familiar with the background information and symbolism of the three constellations that are specifically associated with this Faery Kingdom: Coma Berenice, Leo and Cancer – which represent Gwenevere, her father Leodegrance, and the Kingdom of Lyonesse respectively. Ideally you should be able to locate them in the sky but if you are not able to do this for the time being, having a map of them in your head is the next best thing.

The kingdom of Lyonesse is ruled by King Leodegrance, Gwenevere's father. None of the Faery lands have an exact counterpart in the physical world, and Lyonesse is associated more with the sea than the land, and with the sea of space rather than the salt waters of the ocean. The legends which refer to the submerged land of Lyonesse tend to identify it as the area which now lies between Land's End at the south-western tip of the British Isles and the Isles of Scilly which lie some thirty miles out to sea. As is often the case, these legends and folk-tales are a mixture of comparatively recent history (there seems to have been a disastrously high tide in 1099) some geological evidence of a rise in sea-level several thousand years ago, and the semi-mythological stories of the Arthurian legends.

The sixteenth century historian William Camden noted that the Seven Stones reef which lies off Land's End was also known as 'The City of Lions.' The very names Leodegrance, the City of Lions, Lyonesse, and its French counterpart of Leonais all point us to the archetype of the lion. But there are no lions in Britain, and this Leo is the lion of the stars.

In the ancient Egyptian civilisation, the Sun entered Leo at the time of the inundation of the Nile, which also coincided with the rising of Sirius above the horizon for the first time after an absence of seventy days. Leo was therefore associated with the outpouring of the rich, fertile waters which brought life to the desert lands on either side of the river. In the heavens, the Nile was believed to be mirrored by the Milky Way which fertilised the fields of the stars just as the Nile fertilised the fields of the earth. To this day, the lion's head is traditionally used as a fountainhead, representing the source of life-bringing waters just as Leodegrance is a figure of inspiration and wisdom within the work of the Round Table.

Lyonesse itself is represented by the constellation Cancer which lies directly between Leo's head and the Milky Way. A mysterious and comparatively faint constellation, Cancer has been called the 'gateway of souls' because it occupies the place in the sky where the Sun reaches its highest point in relation to earth, and thus can be said to symbolise the Gate of Heaven. But its ancient association with the crab, that strange creature which lives half in and half out of the water, also brings to mind the primitive life-forms which first crawled out from the deeps onto dry land, bound within the hard form of the encasing shell. In order to reach the starry wisdom of the Round Table you must pass through the birthing pool of Cancer, the Faery kingdom of Lyonesse.

On the other side of Leo is the representation of the star-dusted golden hair which represents Gwenevere, the constellation Coma Berenice. The name refers to Queen Berenice, one of the Ptolemaic Queens of Egypt who reigned between 247–222BC. Legend tells how she vowed to Venus that if her husband returned safely from battle she would cut off her golden hair and offer it to the Gods in thanksgiving. When he did return, she kept her word and placed her shorn tresses in the Temple of Venus. They disappeared, but soon a new constellation was seen in the sky: Venus had taken the Queen's hair and turned it into a cloud of stars. Significantly, this constellation originally formed part of Leo but was later identified as a separate constellation in its own right, just as Gwenevere came into being as the daughter of Leodegrance.

The brightest star in Coma Berenice is called Diadem, another name for the royal crown of a simple band of gold. Diadem is a binary star, which means that it is actually two stars orbiting a common centre of gravity, although as we look at them with the naked eye they usually appear as one. This makes a very interesting link with the tale of the birth of Gwenevere, which describes how two girls, both called Gwenevere, were born of the same mother on the same night. The 'real' Gwenevere could only be distinguished from the 'false' Gwenevere by a small birthmark on her back in the shape of a crown. Gold coins minted in the reign of Queen Berenice depict two stars, and between them a horn of plenty bound with a diadem.

The Journey to Lyonesse, Kingdom of the Stellar Seas

The further you journey into the stars, the more important it is to affirm the connection between yourself and the Sun before you start and when you return. The solar system is our home, and the Sun is the foremost symbol of our identity. You should always conclude your journeys to the stars by passing into the light of the Sun, and instructions on how to do this are given to you at the end of this journey. Take this final section of your journey slowly, otherwise you might feel a bit spaced out and disoriented when you return from the stars.

Before you take this journey you might like to place a representation of the constellations of Leo, Cancer and Coma Berenice on your Round Table. As before, you may find it easier to break the journey up into several shorter sections before taking the full journey.

Journey to the chamber of the Round Table. You can take the whole journey across the lake as before, but you will probably begin to find that after you have visited it a number of times and become familiar with it, you can simply enter into a meditative state of consciousness and take yourself straight to the island, or straight into the chamber of the Round Table itself. See what works best for you, remembering that what actually takes you to any Inner locations is your ability to raise your level of consciousness.

When you are ready, stand before the pale blue veil in the East, and look through to the land that lies beyond.

As the veil dissolves about you, you find that you are looking into a sea-side scene: a beach of white sand, with children playing happily at the edge of a sparkling turquoise sea. It perhaps reminds you of days from your childhood and holidays by the sea. But this is not quite the scene of your own childhood, it is a Faery land which has not been touched by discontent. The scene is lit with a strange, bright light that is not quite sunlight. There are no shadows here. The young children playing in the shallows of the crystal clear water are Faery children.

When you are ready, step through the curtain into the scene which lies before you. Feel the soft white sand beneath your bare toes. See the sparkling waves. Take a deep breath of the clear pure air. You feel as if you are in Paradise.

You watch the Faery children playing at the edge of the water. They are laughing and calling one to another, and their musical voices merge with the sounds of the breaking waves as if soft bells were playing. You see how they relate to the water, as if they are changing the energy of their bodies to resonate with it, as if the water is flowing through them, as if it was part of their life-energy and they were water-babies.

One Faery, a little taller than the others, is standing apart from them and looking out to sea. She seems to know that you are watching her, and turns, and moves towards you, and greets you joyfully. You realise that she is Gwenevere, as a young Faery within her homeland of Lyonesse. She is wearing flowing robes of the palest turquoise-green. Water streams from her golden hair but, strangely, it still looks dry, sparkling like gossamer touched with golden star-dust. She looks younger than you have seen her before, but her years do not correspond to human years and she is wise beyond her apparent age.

She is standing where a stream of milk-water runs down the beach and into the sea. It flows over a bed of tiny white pebbles. She steps into the stream, and begins to walk upwards through its flowing water. She indicates that you should do likewise. You walk over to it. It is running fast over the white polished quartz pebbles, forming tiny whirlpools and eddies which splash into the air and catch the light. You kneel down and dip your hand into it, expecting it to be icy cold. But the water feels like dry, powdery snow flowing past your fingers. You look through the water to the stream-bed but it is hard to gauge the scale of what you are seeing. You can see your hand in the water, and the white pebbles, but they seem to lie a vast distance away, as if the stream bed lay within the stars.

The sound of the water fills your ears. It is like tiny silver bells, ringing faintly but rhythmically. There is an underlying rhythm, a pulsating, as if you are hearing the music of the stars.

Gwenevere continues to walk up the stream, moving effortlessly through the milk-white water. You step into the stream and follow her. You have eyes only for the white stream, and the sparkling quartz pebbles of the stream bed. You carefully watch your step to keep your balance, your eyes on the water swirling past your feet. It has a mesmerising effect. You feel as if you are leaving the earth behind you and walking out into the stars.

The stream broadens out, and its movement becomes slower. You sense that you are nearing its source. You arrive at a deep, wide, circular pool rimmed with smooth, milky white crystal. This pool lies between the worlds, where new life flows into being in an endless stream.

Gwenevere is standing at the edge of the pool. At her side stands her father Leodegrance. He is a tall, proud figure. He is guardian of the Mysteries of this pool which is his kingdom in the stars, the constellation of Cancer, the gateway of souls. His hair is like a lion's mane and glitters with star-fire, his robes glitter with white fire and blue fire, and on his breast is a great jewel like a diamond, sparkling white and ultramarine, the star Regulus at the heart of the lion. He shouts with fierce joy when he sees you, and shakes his great mane of hair so that a shower of shooting stars flies out. He indicates that you should look down into the pool.

As you gaze into its depths, you see tiny translucent creatures, pale, amorphous organisms that drift along with the movement of the water. Whether they are sea-creatures, or distant galaxies, or individual souls about to enter the world, you cannot tell. It is if you are glimpsing the beginnings of the universe.

You wonder where the source of this water might be, and your thought turns to realisation for as you look up you see that at the far side of the pool a white waterfall is tumbling from an immense height. It makes no noise: it falls silently, and in slow motion, and its water sinks into the depths of the pool without ruffling the surface. Where the source of this waterfall is, you cannot tell.

Gwenevere and Leodegrance look at you intently, as if to assure themselves of your focused attention. The atmosphere about the pool begins to heighten. You are aware of the silent slow fall of the water into the pool. A golden mist begins to gather about it, a cloud of the finest droplets which spreads out across the pool. The golden gossamer mist is radiant with light. You realise that it is all about you, touching your cheeks with the most delicate feather-like touch and enfolding you in its gentle grace. The pool, and the waterfall, have become a place of great sanctity and holiness, a place of wondrous light and beauty beyond your imagination, and a source of Mysteries beyond your comprehension.

And now you can see nothing except the golden gossamer mist, but you feel a perfect trust, and contentment. You have reached a place far beyond your knowledge, but you know that all will be well in the light of God.

There is a gentle movement of cold air, and the mist slowly clears. Before your eyes there now opens up the vast extent of the boundless night sky, clear and cold, filled with stars so bright that their glittering light dazzles your eyes. The stars are breathtaking in their beauty, so near and so bright that they almost overwhelm you with their brilliant, shining presence.

You become aware of a great ring of constellations that begins to stand out from the rest of the glittering stars, a circle of shapes and presences that is taking form before your eyes. The Round Table of the Stars is emerging, stretching out into the vastness of the night sky before you. In the farthest distance, you can see the line of the Milky Way, the Winding Waterway of the stars. On its other side lie the most remote constellations of the starry Round Table.

You can begin to pick out the constellations you have learnt to recognise. Immediately to your left is Boötes, a towering figure whose leading star Arcturus shines out warmly with a red-orange glow. Beyond Boötes are the distinctive seven stars that form the Crown of the North Wind. Beyond the Crown lies the elusive figure of Hercules.

You look past this first group of constellations, following round the rim of the Round Table, towards the region of the Summer Stars. Here is the constellation of Lyra with its brilliant blue-white star Vega, the Pole Star of the future. And beyond Lyra is the great white river of the stars, the Milky Way. Above it flies the white swan, Cygnus, its neck and wings outstretched.

And beyond the Milky Way, on the far side of the Round Table, are the human figures of Andromeda, and Perseus. And the third of this group is to their right: Auriga the Charioteer, who is standing in the waters of the Milky Way.

Finally, to your right, as you follow round the complete circle of the rim of the Round Table, you see the constellation of Gemini the twins. Their feet are in the Milky Way but their heads lean together in partnership.

When you are ready, you turn back to find that the golden mist begins to form about you again. As you pause within it, you become aware that the golden mist is becoming warmer, and brighter. Now you can feel the comforting light of the sun's rays shining upon you, familiar, reassuring, warming you to your bones. You have come home to your own place and time, you are fully your Self. Take as much time as you need to make full contact with the light, life and love of the Sun.

Walk through the veil and into the chamber of the Round Table. Gwenevere is seated there, waiting for you. You make your contact with her, and with those who have joined you. You have much to share.

Finally, return to your own place and time. Make sure that you have fully returned into your body and perhaps have something to eat and drink. You have travelled a long way.

CHAPTER NINE

The Faery Kingdom of Oriande

THE FOURTH FAERY KINGDOM is Oriande, the least known and most remote of the five kingdoms connected with Gwenevere. Although the three kingdoms we have studied so far retain a tenuous link with the physical world, Oriande has no connection with any earthly location. But in terms of the Round Table's overall significance and meaning, particularly in regard to its future, Oriande is of crucial importance.

In Oriande, we meet two new members of Gwenevere's family: Madaglan and Jandree. They appear for the first time after Gwenevere has died to the physical world, in order to ask King Arthur what will happen to the Round Table now that she is no longer alive. This is an important question and one we need to consider carefully. What indeed happened to it?

The answer is quite literally in the stars. In effect, Oriande is a kingdom of the stars. It represents all the symbolism contained within the Round Table, set out in the night sky. In the following two chapters you will explore all of the constellations of the Round Table that you glimpsed through the gateway of Lyonesse, and learn how they work together. You will be guided through their traditional attributions and meaning so that you are sufficiently equipped to explore them in your Inner vision, but as always it will be your own personal impressions that will be most valuable to you. The symbol for Oriande is one that you have made yourself, or are in the process of making: your Book of Stars.

MAGICAL CORRESPONDENCES OF THE KINGDOM OF ORIANDE	
Direction:	**North**
Symbol:	**The Book of Stars**
Challenge:	**To develop stellar consciousness**
Gift:	**The Wisdom of the Stars**
Initiator:	**Gwenevere**

Oriande is mentioned only in one version of the Arthurian stories, 'Perlesvaus or The High Book of the Grail.'[1] A long and anonymously written tale, its significance for this study is that it describes the immediate consequences of Gwenevere's withdrawal from the human world. The subject is not dealt with very adequately in the legends as a whole, particularly when we compare it to the evocative descriptions of Arthur's death and his passing across the lake to the Inner world of Avalon. But Faeries do not die as mortals die, and the 'fading' which overcomes them when their time in the human world has come to an end is rarely understood now and certainly does not seem to have been understood by those who recorded Gwenevere's story. The consensus of opinion was that she came to a dishonourable end because of her love for Lancelot and spent her last years in a nunnery as a penitent Christian. Our knowledge of Gwenevere as a Faery reveals this to be very unlikely.

The High Book of the Grail describes the events immediately surrounding Gwenevere's death. In this account, Gwenevere dies of grief after the death of her son Loholt and interestingly this is almost the only indication we have that Gwenevere had a son.[2] Loholt, who is a knight of the Round Table, had just killed a giant in the Perilous Forest but was then himself killed by Kay, who took the credit for killing the giant. After her death, Gwenevere is taken into Avalon. King Arthur, accompanied by Gawain, goes to Avalon to pay his last respects to her. It was Gawain, we remember, who more often than not was responsible for bringing Gwenevere back to the court of the Round Table whenever she had travelled into the Faery realms, and perhaps Arthur relied on him to guide him safely into Avalon.

But on their return to Logres, Arthur found that his land was lying waste and desolate because his Faery Queen was no longer at his side. This is the third example we have so far encountered of the Waste

Land, and in each instance it is clear that the loss of the land's fertility has been caused by the withdrawal of the Faeries, or a representative of their race such as Gwenevere, from the human world. The Waste Land was first described in Boron's account of the journey of the Grail from the Holy Land into Avalon when the land supporting Joseph of Arimathea's company became sterile as a result of the division between human and Faery among his followers. It was caused again by Gwenevere's absence during the three years she spent in Sorelois while King Arthur lived with the 'false Gwenevere.' It is the severance of the connection between the Faeries and the land which causes its lack of fertility. Later, this becomes a crucial issue in the quest for the Grail. The Grail Seeker is shown the Waste Land when he reaches the Grail Castle in Listenois, but if he fails to ask what it means and misses the opportunity to learn about its significance, he is not able to complete his quest. The Grail and the Waste Land are connected at a very deep level.

To return to the story, Madaglan, the Faery King of Oriande and one of Gwenevere's Faery kindred, sends a message to King Arthur to the effect that because the Round Table had originally belonged to Gwenevere it should now be returned to him, Madaglan, because he is her next of kin in Faery. Furthermore, Madaglan tells Arthur, he and Arthur are now at enmity in two respects. First, because Arthur is keeping something that does not belong to him and second, because he rules his land according to the 'New Law.' Madaglan challenges Arthur to renounce the New Law and marry his sister Jandree. If Arthur agrees to these two demands, Madaglan will agree to let Arthur keep the Round Table, and will accept him as a friend and ally.[3]

Jandree is Madaglan's sister and also one of Gwenevere's Faery kindred, although as we have noted, the concept of a Faery family is much looser than that of a human family. Their interest in what will happen after Gwenevere's death seems to extend beyond the immediate future of the Round Table; they are looking to the wider implications of her death in regard to the future of the Faery race within Arthur's kingdom. How will humanity's attitude towards them change, and who will speak for them, now that they are no longer represented by the Faery Queen Gwenevere?

Jandree also sends a message to King Arthur, to ask him to renounce the New Law and worship the god in whom she and those of her kind believe.[4] She says that she would come to Arthur and tell him this herself except that she cannot look upon those who are not of her own faith. She recalls that when the New Law initially came into being, she had to cover her eyes so that she would not be able to see anybody who worshipped the new gods. Fortunately, her own gods had such love for her that they allowed her face and eyes to be uncovered, but to remain without sight. Her brother Madaglan, she says, has vowed to kill all those who follow the New Law, and when he has done so, her gods will restore her sight. Until then, she doesn't want to look at anything!

As is often the case with these strange episodes that make little apparent sense, the words hide the deeper meaning. We need to look at the events following Gwenevere's death through Faery eyes, and when we find ourselves within the Faery realms looking out into the human world we can reach some valuable, if not always comfortable, realisations.

When Madaglan raises the subject of the future ownership of the Round Table he is making a point that would not occur to most people, and certainly does not seem to have been uppermost in King Arthur's mind. As we know, there is much more at stake here than the issue of who inherits a piece of furniture. If this was the only problem, Madaglan would surely not have been in the least concerned about its future, but his urgent concern that it should remain within the ownership of the Faeries gives us further confirmation of the Faeries' continuing close involvement with all that it represented. When Gwenevere died to the human world, the Order of the Round Table lost the principle interpreter of its wisdom. Madaglan's suggestion that Arthur should marry Jandree was an obvious solution: this arrangement would have maintained the vital relationship between human and Faery, and presumably Jandree would also have been able to take on some of Gwenevere's role in guiding the knights through its Mysteries. So far as we can tell from the written accounts of these legends, Arthur was not interested in taking up this proposal, but it is an interesting exercise to conjecture whether or not the Round Table did in fact find its way back into Faery.

The description of Jandree's blindness is another curious episode that makes little apparent sense but repays looking at in more depth. The text describes how she could not bear to look upon those who practiced the New Law, and how her sight was taken from her by her own gods so that she would not have to cover her face and eyes.

Our natural assumption would be that the New Law refers to the conventional Christianity of the Church as opposed to the 'pagan' beliefs of pre-Christian times. But the opening paragraphs of *The High Book of the Holy Grail* set the narrative firmly within the esoteric tradition of the line of Grail guardians that descended from Joseph of Arimathea, and the Christianity of *The High Book of the Holy Grail* is far from orthodox.

But a more fundamental difficulty with equating the 'New Law' with Christianity is that the Faeries have no aversion to Christ, nor to the Grail or its guardians, far from it. The link between Christ and the Grail is as intimate and strong as the link between the Grail and the Faeries. Armed with our knowledge that Madaglan and Jandree are Faeries, it becomes clear that their objection is not to the *religion* practiced within Arthur's kingdom but to the very fact that he is ruling within a human world in which the Faeries are becoming increasingly excluded: this is the 'New Law'. While Gwenevere was living in partnership with King Arthur the link between the two races was preserved, but after her death the likely outcome would be a deepening rift between them, to the detriment of all.

Jandree's need to veil her eyes was not a reaction to Christ or Christianity, and the idea that a Faery has to cover her eyes from Christians really doesn't make sense. It was an attempt to protect herself from the human energies which penetrated her world and an example of the many ways in which the Faeries have to adjust to humanity. To the Faeries, human energies are harsh, abrupt and angular, and the strong imprint these energies make on the delicate world they inhabit is not easy for them to deal with. We might liken the effect to that of a mechanical digger pounding outside our house all day long.

There is a final point to consider in this episode. It is said that Jandree's sight will be returned to her once Madaglan has conquered all those who have adopted the New Law. In other words, this is looking to the distant future of the earth's evolutionary path when the physical world of humankind is once more taken up into the etheric and astral realms of the Faeries. At this time, Jandree and her kind will no longer have any need to protect themselves from humanity because we will be as one, and will see each other with open eyes.

LOOKING THROUGH FAERY EYES

Part of the challenge of Oriande is that you should develop the ability to perceive the world through Faery eyes, something you have already experienced to a certain extent. Once you have mastered the technique of seeing through Faery eyes you will find many opportunities to practice this skill. Best of all, you will be able to look at the stars through Faery eyes, and Gwenevere's dowry of the Round Table, the living and eternal gift to human and Faery alike, will open up in vision before you.

You will find the next three exercises, and those that follow in the next two chapters, to be quite powerful. Don't neglect to maintain your discipline of keeping the outer and Inner worlds quite separate, and always reaffirm your connection with the light and life of the Sun at the end of each meditation. Doing this will not affect your ability to enter into the stellar worlds, and feeling spaced out is not a sign of magical ability!

1. In your Faery Temple or meditation space, relax into a quiet and receptive frame of mind. Now visualise something from the natural world, such as a tree, or a plant, and build it clearly in your mind's eye. When you have it clearly before you, invite Gwenevere to join you in your meditation. Ask for her help in seeing through Faery eyes, and you will find that she comes to stand behind you. Now switch to viewing the same object through her eyes, and observe how different it looks.

    This same exercise can also be practiced out of doors when you walk among trees or in natural surroundings. But don't wander around in a permanent state of seeing through Faery eyes: limit yourself to five minutes or so and then come fully back into your own body.

    When you have made progress with this, you might like to use the same technique from time to time when you are considering any aspect of the relationship between Faery and human.

    When you are ready to finish each meditation, and you may find that it is Gwenevere who indicates when the time is right, break the contact with her by wriggling your shoulders and loosening up the muscles of your neck which may have become a little tense from holding the contact. Visualise Gwenevere turning away from you and fading away into the distance. Thank her for her help, open your eyes, and return fully into your own place and time.

2. Take the journey to the chamber of the Round Table. But instead of exploring the Faery worlds which lie beyond the chamber, ask Gwenevere to show you aspects of the human world which will be revealed to you from where you sit at the Round Table.

3. When you look up at the night sky, look at the stars through your own eyes, and then invite Gwenevere to stand behind you. Look at the stars through Faery eyes.

You can also do this indoors, in meditation. Seated in meditation, bring to your mind's eye a star or constellation that you feel particularly attracted to. Build the pattern of the constellation in your imagination, carefully placing the stars in their correct formation, and then look to see if a figure or pattern is developing amongst the stars. Look at the constellation through your own eyes and wait until you have made contact with its energies.

Then invite Gwenevere to stand behind you. Look at the star or constellation through her eyes. Afterwards, gently break the contact and return fully to your own body.

THE ROUND TABLE OF THE STARS

As we have said, the Kingdom of Oriande represents the continuation of the Order of the Round Table into the future, not only the period immediately following Gwenevere's death but for all those who have taken up its work since then. All the wisdom of the Round Table that was taught to the knights of this Order can be found here, set out in the night sky, as a pattern for eternity.

There are twelve constellations in the Round Table of the Stars. They fall into five groups which although they are not of equal size have equal significance in their depiction of the relationship between Faery and human, and their indication of the way forward into the future. You have already worked with the first group of constellations (Leo, Coma Berenice and Cancer) in your journey to the Kingdom of Lyonesse. Your journey of exploration about the Round Table now continues in the direction indicated by the arrow of Coma Berenice, and the next group you encounter consists of Boötes, Corona Borealis and Hercules. Together, these three constellations form a Temple in which the stellar Mysteries can be contacted and experienced.

BOÖTES

Boötes is the first of this group, a vast kite-shaped figure that covers a large area of the sky in spring. He is the herder and guardian of animals, a vital figure in any culture, and has also been called Atlas, the Bear Driver, the Bear Watcher, the Herdsman, the Lance Bearer and the Shepherd.[5] The composite image of his form is of a giant who holds a staff in his right hand as he strides across the skies. Remember that the best way to locate Boötes is by continuing the curve of the handle of the 'Dipper' (the Great Bear) downwards until you come to the brightest star of the constellation, Arcturus. Arcturus and the Bear thus seem to be closely linked, and the very name Arcturus stems from the Greek word Arktos, which means Bear.

Boötes is the inspiration behind early representations of the Lord of the Animals such as is found on the Gundestrup Cauldron, or in early Celtic tales where he is portrayed as a fierce, protective giant. He is beautifully described in 'The Lady of the Fountain,' one of the tales included in the *Mabinogion*. In this tale, Cynon, who is one of King Arthur's warriors, tells his fellow warriors of how in a journey he had recently made through a forest, he had encountered a giant sitting on top of a mound, wielding a great club, and surrounded by animals. He had asked the giant to demonstrate what command he had over the animals, and by way of response the giant had struck a mighty blow to a stag that happened to be standing nearby, causing the animal to make such a loud roar that all the wild animals of the forest came to gather about him until they were as numerous as the stars in the sky. The giant invited them to graze, and they bowed their heads down before him.[6] The giant is the earthly representation of Boötes, and Cynon had been granted a vision of the Shepherd of the Stars.

Boötes' full authority is recognised in his Chaldean name *Sibzianna*, which means 'Shepherd of the Life of Heaven.' He is active in his watch, striding out across the skies to herd, guide or protect as necessary, just as would a shepherd with his flock.

Boötes' brightest star, Arcturus, sums up and represents the qualities of the constellation as a whole. Arcturus usually shines with a warm orange-yellow light, but if you are lucky enough to catch sight of it as it rises above the horizon after a rain-storm which has cleared the atmosphere you may see it flashing with alternate red and green. When this phenomenon occurs, the quality of the star changes dramatically from a warm, benevolent guardian star to a fiercely active defender of the heavenly creatures.

The useful adage "Arc to Arcturus and speed on to Spica" directs you through the skies from the curve of the handle of the Dipper down to Arcturus and then onwards, continuing in the same arc, to the next bright star which is Spica in the constellation of Virgo. Arcturus therefore acts as a bridge between the Great Bear and the Virgin, transmitting the seven-fold expression of the Divine Wisdom represented by the seven bright stars of the Great Bear towards the Virgin, who gives them form.

JOURNEY TO BOÖTES

The gateway to the Faery Kingdom of Oriande lies in the northern quarter of the chamber of the Round Table.

Make your way to the Round Table as before. Make your contact with Gwenevere and ask her to accompany you, recognising that she continues to interpret the wisdom of the Round Table from the Inner plane kingdom of Oriande, the Faery kingdom of the stars. Stand before the silver veil and reaffirm your connection with the light, life and love of the Sun of our Universe.

When you are ready, pass through the veil. You find that the golden mist of Coma Berenice forms about you as in your earlier journeys to Lyonesse. Be aware that Gwenevere is standing beside you. Allow the presence of Gwenevere, and of the golden mist, to raise your level of consciousness.

When the golden mist fades, the constellations of the clear night sky will open before you, stretching to the furthest reaches of space.

You are standing in the position on the Round Table indicated by the constellation of Coma Berenice. Take your time to visualise the entire circle of the constellations of the Round Table, including the Milky Way and the constellations that lie upon its far side.

Now turn your attention towards the constellation of Boötes to your left. You see the giant figure of the Shepherd of the Stars, holding a staff with his right arm. He is poised to stride out across the fields of the stars to wherever his presence is required.

You become aware of how he cares for every star-creature: the white swan, the eagle, the dragon, the white horse and the Great Bear. See him call to the creatures of the stars, and see how they answer his call. Notice in particular his relationship with the Bear.

When you have done this, ask Gwenevere to help you look at the constellation through Faery eyes. Notice how differently it appears from the Faery point of view. Realise how Boötes relates to Faeries and Faery creatures, and watch as this different world opens up before you.

When you are ready to return, turn about and step back into the cloud of golden mist. Then be aware of the warmth of the Sun penetrating the golden mist. Feel the strength of your solar plexus and of your own identity, your Self. Pass through the veil into the chamber of the Round Table and share your experience with those who have joined you there. When you have fully returned to your own place and time, record your realisations in your Book of Stars.

CORONA BOREALIS, OR THE CROWN OF THE NORTH WIND

The second constellation in this group is Corona Borealis. Like Boötes, it was one of the earliest to be identified and named, and it is one of the most distinctive and easily recognised of all the constellations. It is also one of the few that looks something like its name, and its enclosing, enveloping form with a single distinct entrance has inspired its almost universal association with feminine power.

Greek myth refers to this constellation as Ariadne's Crown, she who saved Theseus from the Minotaur. The Shawnee Indians connect it with twelve star-maidens who came down to earth and danced on the prairie grasslands. One of them married a human man, who after a long and happy marriage with his starry lover eventually took on the form of a white falcon and was thus able to fly freely between the star maidens of the Crown of the North Wind and the white tents of his earthly tribe.[7] This image of the white bird that flies between the stars and the earth is a lovely metaphor for the power of the imagination which allows you to take wings of flight into the stars.

But the most telling association of this constellation is found in Celtic mythology, where it is identified as the Castle of Arianrhod. Arianrhod, whose name means 'Silver Wheel', was the daughter of the Goddess Dôn. Her first consort was Nwyvre, whose name means Sky, or Firmament, and this partnership suggests that Arianrhod is one of the few Faery Deities we can identify with any certainty. The familiar interpretation of her name associates the silver wheel with the Moon but this does not seem entirely convincing: the moon is no more wheel-shaped than any other celestial body, and neither Arianrhod's story nor the location of her castle in the skies makes reference to the Moon. The Bard Taliesin says he was three times in the Castle of Arianrhod, and his three-fold experience reveals it to be an Inner castle of initiation where the symbolic death and rebirth of the initiate can be achieved. This initiation takes you into the wisdom of the stars.

The gateway to this stellar castle is not always open. As the constellation moves through the night sky it turns upon its own axis so that the gap which forms the entrance into the ring of stars does not always point in the same direction. Corona Borealis can thus be seen as the source of the many legends of spinning or turning castles.[8]

JOURNEY TO THE CROWN OF THE NORTH WIND

This constellation is best seen in late spring and summer, and if you have not already located it in the sky you can find it easily from Boötes: it lies just beyond his right arm, as if he was indicating its direction. Nothing can compare with standing beneath the night sky and making your own immediate contact with the stars, but if you are working through this chapter at another time of year, you will find it an easy shape to visualise. You may find it best to take this journey in several stages. Read it through carefully before you start, so that you can easily remember it when you go into this deep meditation.

Begin your journey as before. With Gwenevere, stand before the silver veil. Affirm your connection with the Sun. Pass through the curtain and enter the golden mist. When the mist clears, you find that you are standing in the night sky at the rim of the Round Table, in the position indicated by Coma Berenice. To your left, you see the figure of Boötes, the Shepherd of the Life of Heaven, whose creatures are gathered about him, grazing safely in the fields of the stars.

Beyond him are the distinctive seven stars of the Crown of the North Wind. You realise that they are not still, but are slowly revolving, so that at times they form a complete ring of silver light but then briefly reveal an entrance. They form a castle in the stars, and Boötes is the guardian of the castle.

With Gwenevere by your side, you move easily through the night sky towards the constellation, passing close by to Boötes. As you move towards the seven stars of the Crown of the North Wind you see that as they revolve they are now also expanding upwards, increasing in height until they have grown into seven tall towers of crystalline light, like a shining crown of stars. You pause before the castle, waiting until it turns so that the entrance is before you. When the time is right, you can pass through the entrance. If you are not yet ready, it will move past you, and you can try again at another time.

When you enter the castle, you realise that the seven towers of crystalline light are in fact seven starry beings, Deities of the stellar world, and Deities of the Faery race. They are immensely tall. Their fluid, changing forms are filled with silver light as if of a thousand stars. Watch, and wait, and take your time to experience their energy. It may take you a while to adjust to the very high levels of stellar energy contained within this castle of initiation. You may find that it is sufficient simply to experience this energy. The initiation provided by this stellar castle is very subtle, and takes place entirely within your own consciousness. There may be no outward sign or symbol that the initiation has taken place: it is simply an alteration in consciousness.

Like Taliesin, you may wish to return to the castle on subsequent occasions. And after a while you will begin to experience the particular energy of each of these star-beings. You may begin to experience how each is subtly different from the others. You may perhaps begin to perceive their features, or become aware of different colours within their shining forms. They may begin to teach you of their individual nature, or of their function within the stellar world, although you should not expect that this teaching will necessarily come in the form of words. It is more likely to be experienced as an intuitive knowing, or an understanding, or a realisation of something that you had not understood before.

Remember that Gwenevere is by your side, and will help you see the castle of initiation through Faery eyes. Learn what these Deities mean to her and to those of her Faery kindred. And in turn, you can convey your experience to her so that she can share it with her Faery kindred.

When you are ready to return, wait for the turning entrance to appear before you. Pass out of the castle, move past Boötes who is guarding the creatures outside the castle, and return to the golden mist of Coma Berenice. Then pass through the veil into the chamber of the Round Table, reaffirming your connection with the light, life and love of the Sun. Take your time in returning, and be sure to return completely into your own body, and your own place and time.

You may wish to take this journey several times. The Crown of the North Wind is a castle of initiation, and the process of adapting to its energy, and absorbing it into your consciousness, is unlikely to be achieved in a single visit.

HERCULES, OR THE ONE WHO KNEELS DOWN

The third constellation of this group is another of the earliest constellations to have been identified, but it remains one of the most mysterious. Although it is a large formation, it is not clearly defined and contains few bright or distinct stars. The best way to locate it is to find the bright star Arcturus in Boötes, then mentally draw a straight line from Arcturus through the brightest star of Corona Borealis. Continue the line onwards, and you will arrive in the middle of Hercules. Another way to find it is to locate the bright star Vega in the constellation of Lyra which is the next constellation in the Round Table, and search the area of sky between Vega and Arcturus. Between these two bright stars you may spot what seems to be a backwards letter 'K' with a shape like a box in the middle: this is Hercules! But you will find it much easier to locate it in the sky if you have previously learnt the pattern of its stars. Practice drawing it, and try to memorise its basic shape from all angles so that if it happens to be upside down in the sky when you are searching for it you will have a good chance of locating it.

The widely accepted identification of this constellation as Hercules dates from ancient Greece, where it was associated with the hero of that name who had to overcome a series of challenges usually referred to as the Twelve Labours, many of which involved defeating monstrous creatures such as the Erimanthean Boar and the Stymphalian Birds. These Labours, being twelve in number, have naturally become associated with the twelve signs of the solar zodiac.

But the earlier Sumerian astronomers associated this constellation with their hero Gilgamesh. The epic story of his life, originally entitled 'He Who Saw the Deep', is an account of the adventures of Gilgamesh and his male companion Enkidu. In contrast to Gilgamesh who was a civilized warrior-king, Enkidu was akin to the original Green Man, wild but perfectly at one with nature. The two men became close companions and, like the later Hercules, they undertook a series of challenges that represented the journey and lessons of the human soul. When Enkidu died, Gilgamesh journeyed into the underworld in order to try to understand the mysteries of life, death and immortality.

These are inspiring stories, and it is not easy to understand why a dim and remote constellation has become identified with such major mythological heroes. We might compare it for example with the brilliant and instantly recognisable form of Orion. Hercules looks nothing like a human figure and spends much of his time ignominiously hanging upside down in the sky.

Earlier names for this constellation offer some enlightenment. The Arabic name for it translates as One Who Kneels on Both Knees. The earliest Greek astronomers knew it as *Engonasi,* or One Who Kneels Down. It has also been called Inexplicable Image, One Who Bends Down, Unknown Image and Phantom.[9] Although classical astronomers recognised the importance of this figure and accorded it the status of a hero, the underlying theme is that of a remote presence whose real identity has not yet been fully realised. Its significance lies in its close proximity to the Dragon of the circumpolar stars, the serpent of Wisdom that played a seminal role in the Garden of Eden and consequently in the development of Faery and humankind. The

One Who Kneels Down watches over these events, as if they were frozen in a moment of time, adopting an eternal position of prayer and supplication, and an attitude of infinite humility.[10]

This remote stellar figure can only fully be understood after you have passed through the initiation of the Crown of the North Wind.

JOURNEY TO THE ONE WHO KNEELS DOWN

Before you begin this journey, make sure that you are familiar with the position in the sky of the constellation of the Dragon, whose head lies at the foot of the One Who Kneels Down.

Begin your journey as before, to the chamber of the Round Table. Affirm your connection with the light and life of the Sun, and then pass with Gwenevere through the veil in the North. Enter the golden mist.

When the mist clears, look to your left, to the figure of Boötes and the starry creatures gathered about him. Beyond him lies the Crown of the North Wind. With Gwenevere, you move about the circumference of the stellar Round Table, passing Boötes, and onwards towards the Castle of the North Wind. You wait until the entrance turns towards you, and pass inside. This time, rather than seeking contact with the seven starry beings, you stand at its centre, allowing it to slowly turn about you, aware that it is raising your own level of consciousness as it does so.

When you are ready, you will find that the entrance has moved round, to the opposite side, and from where you stand you can now see the constellation that lies beyond.

You can see the figure of The One Who Kneels Down. Do not move towards this remote figure, but simply observe him from your position within the castle. The figure is kneeling, reverently, as if in deep contemplation. You experience a strange feeling of kinship, as if you can somehow intuit his role in the history, and future, of Faery and humankind.

You can see the constellation of the Dragon, whose body winds between the Great and Little Bears. The dragon's head almost touches the kneeling figure's foot. There is an energy running backwards and forwards between them that is vital to both of them. What is the connection between the One Who Kneels Down, and the Garden of Paradise? Contemplate this Mystery.

Finally, ask Gwenevere to help you to see this constellation through her eyes. And allow her to see it through your eyes.

When you are ready to return, turn around and wait for the castle's entrance to appear before you. Step through it, pass by the figure of Boötes, and return into the golden mist.

Conclude your journey as before, making your connection with the light and warmth of the Sun.

1   Trans. Nigel Bryant, *The High Book of the Grail* (Cambridge: D.S. Brewer, 1978)
2   Ibid, p.175
3   Ibid, p.210
4   Ibid, p.212
5   Gertrude Jobes and James Jobes, *Outer Space: Myths, Name Meanings, Calendars* (New York and London: The Scarecrow Press, Inc. 1964)
6   Gwyn Jones and Thomas Jones, *The Mabinogion* (London, Dent: Everyman's Library, reprinted 1984)
7   Peter Lum, *The Stars in our Heavens* (London: Thames and Hudson, 1952)
8   The question remains as to why the constellation is known as the Crown of the North Wind since it is no more 'north' than any other. The appellation seems to be an indication of its ancient origin. A cave painting discovered in the Cueva di El Castillo (the Cave of the Castle) in Northern Spain shows seven ochre-coloured dots in an almost exact representation of the seven brightest stars of Corona Borealis. The size of the dots corresponds to the brightness of the star, the largest dot representing the brightest star and so on. The drawing is not an exact representation of the constellation's present appearance because it shows the seven stars making a perfect semi-circle, which at present they do not. But because the shape of all the constellations changes slowly throughout the ages, Corona Borealis *would* have been an exact semi-circle during the period 10,000–6,000BC. During this period, the constellation would have been very close to the celestial North Pole and would have been a clear pointer to its location in the sky. It would indeed have been the Crown of the North Wind. Dr Michael A Rappenglück, *Ice Age People find their ways by the stars* (www.infis.org/studies/pdf/mr-2000aenglpdf.pdf)
9   Gertrude Jobes and James Jobes, *Outer Space: Myths, Name Meanings, Calendars* (New York and London: The Scarecrow Press, Inc. 1964)
10 The events that took place in the Garden of Eden are discussed in *Red Tree, White Tree,* Chapter One.

CHAPTER TEN

The Faery Constellations

LYRA, CYGNUS AND THE MILKY WAY

IN THE PREVIOUS CHAPTER, you took the stellar initiation of Corona Borealis, and experienced the significance of the One Who Kneels Down. Together, these form a major stage in your journey about the Round Table of the Stars and you might find it best to take some time over them, perhaps returning to them several times over a period of weeks before you move on.

When you feel ready to continue, the next group of stars you will encounter consists of two constellations that are especially important to the Faeries: Lyra and Cygnus. These constellations depict the essential qualities of Faery in the starry sky, and this quarter of the Round Table is devoted to a pure and joyful experience of Faery. The Milky Way is also included in this group. It is of course an entire galaxy rather than a constellation, but it forms a vital part of the table's overall structure and symbolism.

LYRA

Lyra is one of the smallest constellations in the sky, its visible stars forming two geometrical shapes: a tiny but almost perfect right-angled triangle balanced on one corner of a parallelogram. Its most distinctive feature is its brightest star, Vega, which forms one of the points of the triangle. Vega is very easy to spot in the summer night sky: it is a brilliant blue-white. Together with two other bright stars nearby,

Deneb in Cygnus the Swan and Altair in Aquila the Eagle, Vega forms the so-called Summer Triangle that can be seen high in the eastern sky on summer evenings and lower in the southeast in early autumn.

Vega is also distinguished by being one of the three stars in the northern hemisphere that in turn hold the position of the Pole star, the other two being our current Pole star Polaris, and the star Thuban that lies on the back of the Dragon. Because of the effect of the 'wobble' in the earth's axis, Vega was the northern pole star approximately 12,000 years ago and will be so again in approximately AD 14,000.

Although Lyra's other stars pale beside the brilliance of Vega, the constellation as an entirety holds a great deal of meaning. The early Greeks were responsible for its name, their mythology describing how the god Hermes constructed the first lyre from a tortoiseshell and two horns he discovered on a beach, joining them together with a cross-bar. He made the lyre's strings from the dried tendons he found stretched across the tortoiseshell. Opinions vary as to how many strings he placed on this first lyre but most versions of the legend assume that there were seven. Hermes later gave the lyre to Apollo in exchange for the caduceus that was to become his especial symbol, apparently warning Apollo as he handed over the instrument that although it was capable of creating sounds of great beauty and healing, it would produce only a meaningless cacophony if played by an unskilled hand!

However, the lyre has primarily come to be associated with Apollo's son Orpheus, who perfected its magical capabilities and used its sound to extraordinary effect. It was said that when he was playing the lyre, all of nature stopped to listen, and the sound he created had the power to move stones, change the course of rivers and coax the trees into dance.

Another legend, found in many versions across Asia, also makes a connection between Vega and a stringed instrument, although in this instance the instrument is a weaving loom. The legend tells of the beautiful maiden Chi Nu, the daughter of the Sun king, who is responsible for weaving the sparkling net of the constellations. She weaves with colours not seen on earth: shades of violet, crimson and jewel-green, and she spins shapes of fantastic and miraculous appearance such as chariots pulled by dragons, trailing streamers of cloud. But Chi Nu fell in love with an earthly herdsman, Niu Lang, who consequently neglected his task of looking after the cattle, while

Chi Nu neglected her loom which fell still and silent in the sky. In an attempt to get the work of creation up and running again, the gods came up with the idea of separating the two lovers by placing the Milky Way between them. Chi Nu and Niu Lang were allowed to cross the Milky Way to meet each other only on the seventh day of the seventh (lunar) month of each year.

Although Eastern and Western interpretations of the stars and constellations generally show little resemblance, in this instance they are remarkably similar. The story makes reference to the Milky Way as a symbolic celestial division between the earthly Niu Lang and the star-goddess Chi Nu. The same division was also fundamental to the sacred and magical beliefs of the ancient Egyptians who saw the Milky Way or 'Winding Waterway' as the symbolic division between life on earth and the afterlife among the stars, just as the River Nile separated the realm of the living on its eastern bank from the realm of the dead in the pyramids and tombs on the western bank. The same symbolism is also used in the stellar Round Table, where the Faery constellations of Lyra and Cygnus are separated from the human constellations of Perseus and Andromeda that lie upon the other side of the Milky Way.

And the legends of Orpheus, and of Chi Nu, both reveal the significance of the number seven as a fundamental element of creative energy. The significance of this number touches upon some profound concepts concerning the manifestation of cosmic creative power through all the organisms within our solar system. The absolute creative force is pure energy, but it is easier for us to comprehend if we think of it in terms nearer to our own world, such as colour or sound. The seven-fold manifestation of this creative energy manifests in countless ways and Orpheus had the ability literally to tune into this seven-fold expression of the creative force. By becoming a pure and perfect part of its expression he conveyed that purity of expression to the imperfect material world. Through the medium of sound, he could restore harmony to imperfect and discordant matter.

In our communication with the Faery race and our exploration of their world, one of the best skills we have at our disposal is our awareness of the energies that lie beyond the physical world in light, colour and sound. We have explored some of the possibilities of light and colour, but the constellation of Lyra perfectly expresses the concept of *sound* as an energy on the Inner planes of creation. The constellation lies deep in the silence of outer space but we can tune our consciousness to it with our Inner ear and hear its music if we are able to shut out the noise pollution that daily assaults us, and learn how to *hear*. Lyra symbolises and expresses the qualities of the number seven through the medium of sound.

Faery music is often experienced as strangely powerful and enchanting because of its purity. It is not affected by the limitations of a physical instrument such as an out-of-tune piano or a badly pitched trumpet. Faery 'speech' is equally powerful: it is pure, melodious, and resonates with the sounds of nature. There is nothing intrinsically different between Faery music and human music, but just as the human world is a step further from the Divine state of spiritual purity than the Faeries astral world, so also is human music a step further away from the Divine emanation of pure sound: some of it particularly so! Many tales describe how humans who have caught the sound of a Faery harp or Faery song have been drawn into the Faery realm never to return, or have been so deeply affected by the experience that they have never been the same again.

There is not the space here to explore the creative and healing qualities of sound which can readily be researched elsewhere. But as part of your general approach to the Faeries, try if you can to increase your capacity to *listen*. Just as light pollution obscures our relationship with the stars so also does the equally pernicious evil of noise pollution deaden our ability to really hear. We are accustomed to experiencing 'music' as an unremitting background noise that accompanies our doing something else, rather than experiencing it purely for itself. As a suggestion, play a piece of classical music (rock, pop, jazz etc will not do!) and try to listen to it for ten minutes without allowing your attention to wander. Listen only to the sound, concentrate your attention only on the actual notes as they rise and fall, listen to the sound quality, the shape of the melodies, the way the notes are combined and interweave, the patterns and the colours that are evoked. You will find it an experience akin to meditation, but perhaps even more inspiring. And just as you have learnt to perceive the Faeries' shapes and forms within the pure colour that you envisioned in Chapter Three, so you may come to realise how they can also manifest within pure sound.

JOURNEY TO LYRA

As with most of these Inner journeys, it is suggested that you might like to read the whole passage through a couple of times before you start so that you can easily bring it to mind during your meditation.

Begin your journey as before and travel to the chamber of the Round Table. Make your connection with the Sun. With Gwenevere, pass through the silver veil in the north, and enter the golden mist.

When the mist clears, you can see the constellations of Boötes, the Crown of the North Wind, and The One Who Kneels, as the rim of the Round Table stretches round to your left. But this time, you set your gaze on the more distant group of Lyra, Cygnus and the Milky Way in the region of the Summer Stars. Lyra is the first of these.

You may at first be aware of the brilliant blue-white star Vega. And then you see the rest of the constellation unfolding about it. You might perceive it either as a geometrical form of a small triangle balanced upon a parallelogram, or as a seven-stringed lyre or a harp, depending on which image appeals to you most. When you have located it and visualised it clearly, you will find that you can move towards it simply by expressing your desire to do so.

As you approach Lyra, you become aware of the utter silence of space, a silence such as you rarely experience in your everyday life. You reach out with your Inner perception and try to comprehend the vastness of the silence. The silence is profound and fathomless. You strain your ears to try to catch the faintest sounds at the furthest reaches of the night sky. You listen to the stars.

You see that the strings of the lyre are gently moving in the winds of space. You know that a sound is being produced, and it is so pure and clear that you cannot relate it to any earthly music.

You are drawn towards it. You can see the seven strings. You become aware that each of them produces a different quality of sound. You pause for a while to experience this.

The lyre conveys a perfection of tone and balance which expresses a creative energy so pure and high that it heals everything it touches. You allow yourself to enter into the sound, until you are filled by it. You become aware of each of the seven strings resonating within you.

And now you realise that you can *see* the sound, and that it is creating wonderful forms in the sky, amongst the stars. These fluid shapes and patterns, swirling clouds of colour and light, flow out from the strings, full of colour and beauty, an expression of the sound that creates them. You can become a part of this. *You can become the lyre.*

After a while, as with all Nature, you come to a pause. You reach a moment of absolute stillness...

When you are ready, turn to Gwenevere who is beside you, and realise that she is eager that you should also perceive and experience the sound of the lyre as it is experienced by the Faeries.

She begins to move among the changing patterns of light, and together you experience this outpouring of star energy where light, colour and sound are as one.

THE MAGICK OF THE RHYME

Dance joyfully with lightest foot
across the midnight sky.
And whisper with the harmonies
That gather there to fly.

Hold strong that note, tremendous rung,
bright stars in sky's embrace.
Entwined with threads of moonlight spun,
within this Sacred Space.

For circles round of spirals made,
and words and bells doth chime.
At trancing hour our hearts uplift,
the Magick of the Rhyme.

Dance joyfully with flight of foot,
God's Glories to partake.
Cast shimmering light, beneath the moon,
to sparkle in our wake.

Encircle now this stillness Maked
and fling thy tokens high.
Hold out thy hand, and clasp within
the meaning and the why.

What golden mist, with wanton air,
doth play upon this Earth?
In love and laughter bring forth now,
exquisite in her mirth.

Come brothers, sisters, dance with me,
Glad hearts of folk so fey.
Roused melodies, in charmed delight,
seductive notes to play.

In dreaming wake, of conscious fate,
Pray welcome, One and all.
Twixt day and night, Love's gift invites
All-comers to the Ball.[1]

When you are ready, return as before. The further you journey into the stars, the stronger should be your contact with the Sun on your return.

CYGNUS THE SWAN AND THE MILKY WAY

The second of the Faery constellations is the White Swan: Cygnus. Cygnus is one of the few groups of stars that looks something like its name, and the distinct cross-shaped formation that soars above the Milky Way is easily recognisable as a swan's outstretched neck and wings.

The constellation is also sometimes called the Northern Cross because of its shape, and it mirrors a similar shaped constellation in the southern hemisphere known as the Southern Cross. Deneb, its brightest star, forms part of the Summer Triangle, but the constellation is visible from May until September from most northern latitudes. If you have difficulty in locating it, it is one of the many constellations that can be located from the Great Bear or Dipper. Find the two inner stars of the 'dipper' (that is, not the two you use to locate the Pole star,) draw a line through them and continue the line for some distance. You will eventually reach the star Albireo which lies at the base of the outstretched neck of Cygnus. Deneb marks the tip of the swan's tail.

There is not a great deal of mythology connected with this distinctive constellation, which is surprising when we bring to mind how striking and beautiful a presence the bird is in our landscape and mythology. The legend pegged onto it by the early Greek civilisation makes only a weak association, relating it to Cycnus, a musician-king and friend of the hot-blooded Phaeton who fell from the sky in his father's sun chariot and plunged into a river. Cycnus dived into the river to try to find him, a brave action which nonetheless so incensed the Gods that they changed him into a swan for his efforts. Apollo took pity on him and sent him into the sky.

There is, however, a great deal of interesting lore and mythology connected with the swan that for some reason has not yet become associated with its stellar counterpart. Swans have many intriguing qualities about them, not least that they almost always mate for life and therefore readily symbolise fidelity. In Indian legend the swan is said to possess the ability to separate milk from water, so that if offered a drink from a mixture of the two liquids it will drink only the milk. As with Lyra, Cygnus is also expressive of the creative power of sound. The name *swan* comes from a root word meaning sound, or to sing. The phrase 'swan song' refers to the belief that just before it dies, the Mute Swan is able to find its voice and to produce a single beautiful melody.

But above all, the power and purity of this great white bird makes it a perfect symbol of the Faery race. The swan is a symbol of the Faeries' *strength*, and it is important that we should understand what is meant by this. In the physical world we define strength as the ability to exert a force against a physical resistance, but this definition lacks meaning in the Faery realm where there are no physical bodies. In their astral world, strength is connected with *lack* of resistance; it is the Faeries' capacity to receive, hold and transmit energy that is an indication of their strength. Strength in the Inner worlds is akin to what we call 'power' in the physical world but with the additional quality of spiritual purity. The greater the spiritual purity, the greater the power. The great white birds that travel vast distances across the globe in their annual migration – the crane, the ibis, the white goose, the swan – are all symbols of a spiritual strength and purity that is honoured in many world mythologies. The celestial Swan represents all of these in its perpetual flight along the white waters of the Milky Way that carry it away from our familiar skies and into the unknown regions beyond the Summer Stars.

The story of the Children of Lir perfectly illustrates how the white swan has become such a poignant symbol of the Faery race.[2] The Faery King Lir was one of the most anciently revered of the Faery race of Ireland known as the Tuatha dé Danaan or Children of the Goddess Danu. He had four Faery children, Fionnuala, Fiacra, Conn and Aodh, who were changed into swans by their jealous step-mother Aoifa. (It's interesting to note the similarity between this name which is pronounced 'eee-fah', and Eve.)

Even as swans, the Faery children retained their sense of Faery self: they retained their power of speech, and they were given the ability to create songs more beautiful than any other in the world. But they were doomed to spend three hundred years on each of three lakes that put an increasing distance between them and their Faery father, while offering them only a cold and hostile environment: Lake Darvra, the narrow Sea of Moyle, and the Western Sea that had no bounds except the sky.

Their exile only came to an end at a moment signalled (according to different versions of the story) by the sound of a bell, by the appearance of a Druid from over the seas, or the marriage between a king from the North and a queen from the South. When, after nine hundred years as swans, they eventually regained their Faery form, they found that their father had long gone, and that his bright house, his white hounds and his bright-maned horses had also completely disappeared. The time of the Faery race had long since passed away.

For those who retain the memory of an existence as Faery, this story can be almost unbearably poignant in its description of what it is like to experience exile in the human world, where the passage of years seems to bring an increasing sensation of bleakness and isolation from all that is real, along with the fear that the Faery world might never be regained.

JOURNEY TO CYGNUS AND THE MILKY WAY

Begin your journey to the chamber of the Round Table as before. Reaffirm your connection with the Sun, pass through the silver veil, and move into the golden mist with Gwenevere.

When the mist clears, you see Boötes, Corona Borealis and The One Who Kneels Down, circling about the rim of the Round Table to your left. Beyond them is Lyra with its brilliant blue-white star Vega. You move past them, and easily cover a great distance of the night sky towards your destination of Cygnus and the Milky Way.

You hear the sound of the lyre playing softly, and allow its healing harmonies to strengthen you…

And now you see the Milky Way stretching out across the celestial Round Table: a white river of glittering stars. And you see the great white swan flying over it, its wings outstretched, beating silently in the cold air. The swan and the white waters seem to be one: the movement of the swan, and the movement of the river. And yet there is a paradox: each appears to be flowing into the vastnesses of space and yet at the same time it remains fixed, immovable in its relationship to the constellations that surround it. The swan symbolises the soul of the Faery race: its strength, its future, and its predicament.

You ask Gwenevere to allow you to see the Swan through Faery eyes. And you allow her to see the Swan through your eyes.

When you are ready, you turn about, travel back across the Round Table and into the golden mist of the constellation of Coma Berenice. Pass through the silver veil, and reaffirm your connection with the light, life and love of the Sun.

This concludes your journey through the Faery constellations of the Round Table of the Stars.

1   The poem 'The Magick of the Rhyme' is reproduced with kind permission of the author, Melanie Miller-Wells.
2   Ella Young, *Celtic Wonder Tales* (Dublin, Maunsel and Company, 1910) reprinted (London, Abela Publishing, 2010)

CHAPTER ELEVEN

Beyond the Milky Way

S O FAR, YOU HAVE EXPLORED two groups of constellations in the Round Table of the Stars. The first group, consisting of Boötes, Corona Borealis and the One Who Kneels Down, forms a temple of the stellar Mysteries that has equal relevance for human and Faery. In this group, you learnt of Boötes as the Shepherd of the Creatures of Heaven, who stands guard before the Castle of the North Wind, in which you experienced an initiation into the Stellar Mysteries. This enabled you to move on towards an understanding of the significance of the third constellation of this group: the One Who Kneels Down.

The second group of stars consists of Lyra, Cygnus and the Milky Way, and this group is especially linked to Faery.

The next group that you will encounter in your journey about the Round Table of the Stars consists of the constellations of Andromeda, Perseus and Auriga. Within the overall symbolism of the Round Table, this group represents humanity. These constellations lie on the far side of the Milky Way and they have a very different feel to them, as you will soon begin to experience for yourself.

THE SEAT OF HUMANITY: ANDROMEDA AND PERSEUS

These constellations are best seen in October and November evenings. The easiest way of locating them is from Cassiopeia, which is one of the nearby circumpolar constellations. The distinctive 'W' shape of Cassiopeia can be seen high in the north-eastern sky in October. One point of the 'W' indicates Perseus, and the other point indicates

Andromeda. But these are two of the least distinctive star groups in the sky, and neither of them looks very much like a human figure.

According to Greek legend, Princess Andromeda was the daughter of Queen Cassiopeia and King Cepheus, who is also seen in one of the nearby circumpolar constellations. Queen Cassiopeia boasted that she and her daughter were more beautiful than either Hera the Queen of Heaven, or the Nereids, a group of Sea-Goddesses. The Nereids took offence at this and complained bitterly to Poseidon, the God of the Sea. In order to pacify them and punish Cassiopeia for her bragging, Poseidon threatened to send a sea-monster, Cetus, to devour Cassiopeia and Cepheus's people, and destroy their land.

The king and queen were understandably rather upset by this, and appealed to an Oracle for guidance as to what they should do about it. The Oracle advised them that their land and people could be saved, but only if they were happy to offer their daughter Andromeda as a sacrifice to Cetus. They agreed to this somewhat drastic solution and Andromeda was duly chained to a rock at the ocean's edge to await her fate. The image has inspired numerous artists to interpret the scene as an erotic image graced by a tasteful veneer of classicism.

However, the hero Perseus, fresh from killing the Gorgon Medusa by cutting off her head, and by chance passing by Andromeda's rock on his return home, came to her rescue. Things didn't go too well to start with; a lot of blood was spilt, but Cetus only grew stronger. Then Perseus had the good idea of holding up the Medusa's head, which he fortunately happened to have with him. The gaze of the Gorgon's eyes turned the monster Cetus to stone. Andromeda was saved, Perseus managed a few more good deeds on his way home, and as a reward he was allowed to marry Andromeda. She had actually been promised to her uncle Phineus, but he also fell under the gaze of the Gorgon's head and was conveniently turned to stone in the nick of time.

The legend contains little that appeals to us. The Gods' behaviour can hardly be called Divine, and the boasting, jealousy, anger, complaining, retribution and cruelty with which they conduct their lives seems to present a catalogue of the worst manifestations of the human shadow rather than an ideal to which we might aspire. Neither is there much that appeals to us in the story of Perseus's dramatic rescue of Andromeda and his display of bravery in vanquishing Cetus and a miscellany of monsters. It is difficult for us to relate either to the hapless victim Andromeda or to the impossibly heroic Perseus.

Perseus was certainly favoured by the Gods, who lavished him with every possible encouragement and a bagful of magically empowered artefacts to help him carry out his good deeds, but his story seems so much larger than life that it is difficult to connect it with the humdrum challenges of our own daily lives.

Nevertheless, the human condition is undoubtedly represented here, and however we might search the stars for a more flattering representation of ourselves we inevitably arrive at Perseus and Andromeda. Here are Everyman and Everywoman, and here are our struggles against what seem to be overwhelming odds, whether the forces of nature that we prefer not to heed or understand, or the internal forces of our own shadows. There can be no doubt that we are currently experiencing a huge increase in elemental energies of the very kind that Poseidon threatened would engulf the land of Cepheus and Cassiopeia: earthquakes, tidal waves and hurricanes. All these are found in the story of Perseus and Andromeda, alongside our persistent tendency to blame others for such misfortunes.

The archetypes of this story represent humanity at the stage of rebellious youth, lacking independence and reluctant to take responsibility. If we continue in our present course we will all become Andromeda, powerless to resist the rising tides of the devouring sea which threatens to drown us and our world. There is some irony in the fact that the name Andromeda can be translated as 'ruler of men.'

Moving on to Perseus, legend tells that he was the son of the immortal God Zeus and the mortal woman Danae. But the constellation which bears his name contains a fatal flaw: the star Algol, which is generally considered to be the most malefic in the sky. It is often referred to as the Winking Demon, a reference to the fact that its brightness fluctuates every 2-3 days. It is actually a binary or double star, and its apparent loss of light occurs when the dimmer of its two stars passes in front of the brighter. The name derives from the Arabic *Ra's al Ghul*, meaning the Demon's Head. The Hebrews called this star *Rosh ha Satan*, Satan's Head, and saw it as Adam's first wife, Lilith.[1] The Chinese gave it the even more dismal name of Piled Up Corpses. Tolkien may also have made reference to this star in *The Lord of the Rings* as the evil eye of Sauron whose baleful influence spread over much of Middle Earth.

Greek mythology identifies the star Algol with the head of Medusa. The myth of Medusa is now permanently linked with the victorious

Perseus who killed her by cutting her head from her body, but sadly her origins and history up until her transformation into a Gorgon are now almost entirely forgotten. She was one of three sisters, and was known far and wide for the beauty of her magnificent long hair. One day when she was worshipping in the Temple of Athena, she was ravished by Poseidon, whom we have already encountered in connection with Andromeda. Athena was so enraged at this that she transformed Medusa into a Gorgon, changed her beautiful hair into scorpions, and cursed her to turn people into stone whenever she looked at them, even after her death.

When we give thought to the meaning of this unhappy sequence of events (what was Poseidon doing in Athena's Temple and why wasn't he punished?) we can't help but arrive at the conclusion that Medusa is another of the hapless victims in this story. This makes Perseus's triumphant display of her decapitated head all the more discomforting. Medusa was not evil, but suffered a violent punishment for being overpowered by Poseidon when she was at prayer. Even worse, her reputation was corrupted for eternity while Poseidon, we cannot help but notice, escaped without a slur on his character. Our inevitable tendency is to regard Algol/Medusa as an indication of the virtuous Perseus's triumphant victory over evil, but this is far from the truth, and again we can only feel unease at the events described in this story.

JOURNEY TO ANDROMEDA AND PERSEUS

Before you begin your journey to these constellations, study the shape of them until you can remember them easily and are able to picture them in your mind's eye. Neither of them is a very convincing likeness of a human, particularly Andromeda who looks a more like a tentatively drawn stick-figure. But if you study the pattern of the stars of Perseus carefully and let your imagination guide you, you may find that you can re-draw his figure in a more convincing human likeness. This is a talismanic act in itself, and although there is usually a traditional way of joining up the stars in a constellation, there is no reason why the customary pattern should be the only possible interpretation. The stars are evolving, as are we. These constellations that represent the human race are indeed as yet poorly defined, but the simple act of visualising them in a positive way and strengthening their images in your mind's eye is a valuable achievement that will have real, magical power.

You may prefer to take the following journey in two separate stages, the first journey taking you to the near bank of the Milky Way, and the second journey taking you across the Milky Way to stand on the far side.

Begin your journey as before, taking yourself in your imagination to the chamber of the Round Table where you make your contact with Gwenevere and all those who join you. When you are ready, affirm your connection with the light, life and love of the Sun, and then pass through the silver veil and enter into the golden mist of the constellation of Coma Berenice. Gwenevere accompanies you.

When the golden mist clears, wait until you can see the entire Round Table of the stars stretching out in the night sky about you. To your left are Boötes, Corona Borealis and the One Who Kneels Down. Continuing about the rim of the Round Table you see the stars of Lyra with its brilliant blue-white star Vega, and the constellation of Cygnus the white swan flying over the Milky Way.

Focus your attention on the Milky Way, the river of stars which flows across the expanse of the Round Table from one side to the other. With Gwenevere by your side, you effortlessly move towards it across the vast expanse of the night sky, orienting yourself by the constellations that you have learnt so far.

When you reach its bank, pause to observe the millions of stars and constellations that are flowing past you in their ceaseless round. For the moment, you are content to stand on the bank with Gwenevere and watch this wonderful vision.

When you are ready, look over to the other side and build in your imagination the constellations that you can there. You see two figures, the starry representations of Andromeda and Perseus. You are aware of their stories. You see Andromeda, powerless against the cosmic tides.

You see Perseus, holding up the head of Medusa. You know that they represent humanity, man and woman, and the qualities and attributes of humankind. Be aware of the feelings that rise within you, whether they are of hope or despair, compassion or denial... Do not look for easy answers or search for solutions but stay with your feelings. If you find the figures difficult to visualise or connect with, simply observe that difficulty.

Be aware of Gwenevere standing by your side. And now look at the same two figures through Gwenevere's eyes. Understand how she views them, and take heed of whatever thoughts or realisations come into your mind, whether or not you find them easy to accept. You may find that you reach a new understanding about the relationship between Faery and human, not only in the past and present, but for the future.

Above all, find it in your heart to relate to these two constellations with *compassion*.

Finally, when you are ready, cross over the Milky Way. You can do this simply by expressing the desire to do so. Take this part of your journey slowly, and enjoy the experience: it is an integral part of the Round Table.

Then, stand with Gwenevere upon the far bank, with Andromeda and Perseus.

Experience what this feels like.

Look out over the entire Round Table from this position, which is directly opposite to Coma Berenice. Be open to any thoughts or realisations that come to you regarding the relationship between humanity and the Round Table of the stars.

When you are ready to return, cross back over the Milky Way (it is important not to omit this stage) and head for the golden mist of Coma Berenice which will feel comfortingly familiar to you. Pass through the mist and return through the veil into the chamber of the Round Table. Do not forget to reaffirm your connection with the light, life and love of the Sun. You have journeyed a long way. Think about what you have seen and experienced, and write your realisations in your Book of Stars.

INTO THE FUTURE: AURIGA

You may have found that the previous journey left you with some
unanswered questions, or the impression of unfinished business.
Certainly there is little in the story of Perseus and Andromeda that
appears to inspire or offer much hope. But the evolution of humankind
and our relationship to the Faeries is surely unfinished business on a
grand scale!

Auriga, the third constellation in this section of the Round Table,
is one of the most enigmatic of all the groups of stars although it has
been recognised in its present form for thousands of years. It offers
a sign, written large above our heads, of the way forward from the
apparent impasse represented by the previous two constellations.

Auriga consists of only five bright stars, which form an approximate
pentagram. This constellation can best be seen in the northeast in the
late autumn and early winter months. Its most distinctive star is the
bright and beautiful creamy-white star Capella, and if you can locate
Capella you will easily pick out the rest of the pentagram. Curiously,
one of Auriga's five stars is shared with the constellation of Taurus the
Bull, and without this extra star Auriga could scarcely be said to form
any recognisable shape at all. Taurus lies to the southeast of Auriga,
with a distinctive 'V' shaped group of stars representing the head and
horns of the bull. The last star in top of the V is *El Nath*, which is also
the fifth star of Auriga.

The ancient Greeks regarded this constellation as a representation
of Erichthonius, an early King of Athens who invented the four-horse
chariot. As a reward for his gift to mankind, Athena placed him in the
stars as the constellation Auriga, but there seems little scope among its
mere five luminaries for the depiction of either a chariot or the four
horses that draw it. Yet the Chinese astronomers called it *Five Chariots
of the Five Emperors*, which suggests a world-wide recognition of this
constellation as a horse-drawn vehicle driven by a powerful figure
of authority. The mystery is compounded by the fact that although
Auriga has no visible horses he does carry three goats, one in his left
arm nestling against his shoulder, and two kids which rest in his lap.
His small passengers must surely impair his driving skills!

The statue of the Charioteer at Delphi sheds some light on the
mystery, and the correspondences between this statue and the
constellation are remarkable. The stone Charioteer also has neither

horses nor chariot but stands poised and confident, holding the reins of his unseen horses in one hand with an air of unruffled serenity. He is the epitome of one who has achieved perfect authority over the animal instincts which are represented by the horses over whom he has such perfect control. He has literally harnessed their power, and is able to direct it to good use as he races along his destined path.

The key to this mystery is to realise that the chariot, goats and horses are all aspects of the man. Without the power of the passionate instincts and the fundamental human urge for fight or flight, the Charioteer will make no headway. It is our ability to harness the power of our instinctual drives that make us whole, and without the horsepower, the chariot which represents the 'physical vehicle' of the body can make no progress. If, on the other hand, the horses are allowed free rein they will run wild; the Charioteer will have no control over himself and his journey through life but will be pulled hither and thither at the whim of the wild animals that drag him along.

We might also think of the four horses as symbolic of the four elements of air, fire, water and earth, again indicating the charioteer's command over the forces of nature. And the pentagram or five-pointed star is in itself widely recognised as the fundamental symbol for a human figure, a geometrical representation of the five points formed by the hands, feet and head.

Here, as we reach the penultimate constellation in our journey about the Round Table, we see the perfect pattern of the Rose Cross made manifest in humanity. The four elements or points of the cross over which Auriga the Charioteer has perfect command are represented by the four unseen horses. We can also see these elements displayed in his starry environment. He has his feet in the waters of the Milky Way, and his head is in the airs of space. He is 'fired' by the horsepower that drives him and he is at one with the earth of the physical vehicle that surrounds and protects him. If the constellation of Auriga contained only four stars it would hold little meaning, but the addition of the fifth star, uniquely drawn to our attention through its shared status with another constellation, transforms an otherwise unremarkable asterism into a powerful symbol of evolved humanity.

The goats complete the picture by giving heart to the man, and as we have often seen before, the brightest star of the constellation reveals the meaning of the whole. The beautiful creamy-white star Capella, the sixth brightest in the sky, is named after the Latin for

She-Goat. The name refers to the legend of Amalthea the sacred goat, who nursed the infant Zeus with the milk of the stars. Capella rests over the heart of the Charioteer, and completes the symbolism of the man who has harnessed the power of his instinctual passions, drives forward to follow his own destiny and, with the sacred mother of God represented at his heart, has become a fully realised spiritual being. The twin kids which rest in his hand represent the infant humanity, the precious burden he carries in his journey through the universe. And they also, of course, simply represent themselves, as part of the animal kingdom which is so closely linked with our own evolution.

A final point of significance is that Auriga stands as a bridge over the Milky Way. Unlike the swan whose flight is irrevocably linked with the movement of the galactic waters, the Charioteer has found the way to cross over them: he can move freely, and at will. He represents the way forward for humanity, but the significance of his journey is not for humanity alone. When all humankind becomes as the Charioteer and discovers its ability to move onwards and upwards from the confines of the earth and its own lower nature, this evolutionary step forward will affect humanity, Faeries and creatures alike. The Faeries cannot move forward without us, and until all humanity, or at least a good portion of it, has shifted its consciousness beyond the physicality of the earth, the Faeries cannot look to a future beyond the earth, and they have little control over what that future might be.

From our human point of view, the health and vitality of the Faery race and the etheric/astral world they inhabit is an infallible indication of the health and vitality of the physical earth, just as the health of the human physical body is indicated by the state of the etheric body. As we have seen throughout this book, our ancestors understood that the Sacred King derives his power and authority from his relationship with a Faery Priestess who represents the whole earth. When this relationship is severed, the physical land loses its vitality and becomes a Wasteland, just as when our etheric body becomes depleted in energy our physical body becomes diseased.

The analogy becomes even more significant when we realise how the Faeries are affected by our destruction of the physical earth. It has an effect on them that is equivalent to the injury our bodies suffer from external, physical causes. When severe injury happens to the physical body, the etheric body is traumatised. Its healing can only take place through the renewal which is brought into it via the more subtle bodies. We cannot underestimate the difficulties we cause the Faeries by our wilful destruction of the planet they are so inextricably linked with. Just as the etheric body is tied to the physical, so are the Faeries tied to the Earth until the Earth changes.

This does not mean that the future is hopeless for the Faeries, but time is certainly running short, and their increasingly urgent attempts to make contact with those of us who can hear their voices are testimony to their present dire situation. When we become aware of the Faeries, acknowledging and believing in them, taking them into our consciousness and allowing them to benefit from the best that we may be, we provide them with a means whereby they too can bring about changes to their consciousness, and we can grant them the ability to move forward.

JOURNEY TO AURIGA

Before you journey to Auriga, make sure that you have a clear picture of what this figure looks like. You only have five stars to work with! But in meditation, hold them in your mind's eye and see what begins to take shape. Practice doodling with them on paper, and formulate an image for this constellation that is appropriate to its symbolism, that appeals to you, and that you can clearly visualise. You may arrive at something that bears little resemblance to the conventional image of this constellation, but that is all to the good. This exercise in itself will have a magical effect.

When you are ready, begin your journey as before. Make your contact with Gwenevere, affirm your connection with the Sun, and step through the veil into the golden mist. When the mist clears, wait until the entire Round Table builds clearly in your vision. The stars circling round to your left are bright and clear against the night sky. The white river of the Milky Way lies in the distance. You can see the constellations of Andromeda and Perseus on the far side.

But this time your destination is Auriga, and you can see the Charioteer, in the form that you have created for him in your mind's eye, confident, calm and sure, holding the reins of his four horses as he makes speed across the waters of Milky Way. You are aware of the balanced and controlled power that allows him to retain his steady position within his chariot. You are aware that he has the ability to bridge the Milky Way and that he is equally at home on either of its banks.

Gwenevere is standing at your side. You realise that the identity and purpose of the Charioteer may be as much a mystery to her as to you. And yet, perhaps Gwenevere is aware of what the human race is capable of achieving, for its own self and for the Faeries. See Auriga through her eyes and try your best to understand all that is shown and told to you. Allow her, in turn, to see Auriga through your eyes.

In order to fully experience and demonstrate what Auriga signifies, you might like to take on his form. If you wish, imagine that you are standing poised in the chariot that is speeding across the white waters of the Milky Way. You know that it is only your own determination that keeps it upright. In your right hand you hold the reins of a team of four powerful horses, and the transmission of their power through the reins into your hands is so strong that you feel as if you have harnessed their power within you.

Make an assessment of how well you are managing, and notice how your horses and chariot are behaving. Is your chariot balanced, or wobbling from side to side? Do you have the horses under control, or are they headstrong, with the bit between their teeth? Do you know where you are going, or have you relinquished that decision to the horses? Or, perhaps, you do not know exactly where you are going but you trust that all is going according to the Divine Plan.

Turn your attention to the she-goat against your left shoulder. Why is she travelling with you?

Turn your attention to the starry forms of Andromeda and Perseus to your right. As the Charioteer, how do you relate to them?

When you are ready, step down from the chariot and onto the bank of the Milky Way. You can see the golden mist of Coma Berenice in the distance. You move towards it swiftly and easily; you step into the golden mist, and pass through into the sunlight. When you have shared your realisations with those who join you within the chamber of the Round Table, return to your own place and time.

This completes your journey through the group of constellations which represent the place of humanity at the Round Table of the Stars.

GEMINI: THE SIEGE PERILOUS

The final place at the Round Table of the Stars consists of a single constellation: Gemini, the celestial twins. This constellation marks the culmination of your journey and brings you back nearly full circle to where you began, in the constellation of Cancer. It is only between the constellations of Gemini and Cancer that the circle of the Round Table coincides with the circle of the solar zodiac.

The twins have their feet in the Milky Way, but their faces are turned towards a vast expanse of sky which contains no bright stars and only one recently identified constellation, Lynx.[2] You can best locate Gemini from the Great Bear or Dipper, where you will find the two brightest stars of Gemini, Castor and Pollux, opposite the two 'marker' stars of Merak and Dubhe.

Although Gemini also forms part of the solar zodiac, its meaning within the Round Table is very different to that of popular astrology. In the symbolism and meaning of the Round Table, Gemini represents the coming together of all that you have learnt and experienced so far, and it is the culmination of your work in the stars. It represents the concept of twins, of mirroring, of the relationship between the human and Faery races and their different worlds. And it represents the two aspects of the Christ: the White Christ of Faery and the Christ who became Man. Auriga points the way forward for humanity, but in Gemini we see what we may become when our journey is completed, and thus within the Round Table of the stars it symbolises the perfected being who will one day rightfully occupy the mysterious empty seat at the Round Table called the 'Siege Perilous.'

In the Arthurian legends, the name of each of the knights was inscribed upon their seat at the Round Table, but one seat remained empty, and had no name on it. This place was the Perilous Seat. Much has been written about this seat, but it is important to distinguish between the few facts that we have at our disposal and the later superstition that has grown up about it. The Perilous Seat first appears in Robert de Boron's *Merlin* that we have discussed in some detail in Chapter Two. Merlin, who is explaining the meaning of the Round Table to Uther PenDragon, describes how the seat was first created at the Round Table that was made by Joseph of Arimathea. Joseph, who was following instructions given to him by Christ in a vision, placed the Grail, and the fish that had been caught by the Fisher King, on his table. He then took his own seat at his table, in the place that represented the seat originally taken by Christ at the table of the Last Supper. He asked Bron, the Fisher King, to sit at his right hand. Bron did so, but then moved one seat away. The seat that he had vacated, indicated the place that had been left by Judas Iscariot when he left the table of the Last Supper. This place, it was said, would only be filled by Bron's grandson.[3]

The story is curious in its detail, and seems to highlight some particular, almost ritual significance, in Bron's action of sitting next to Joseph, and then getting up and moving away to create an empty seat. But putting this aside, this explanation of the origin and meaning of the Perilous Seat as the place once occupied by Judas Iscariot is now commonly accepted. One of Joseph's companions, the hapless Moyse, decided to take the seat for himself but the earth opened up beneath him and he fell into an abyss.

However, when Merlin later repeats the same story for the benefit of King Arthur, he says that the empty seat represented the place originally taken by *Christ* at the table of the Last Supper.[4] So we have two very different explanations of the origin of the Perilous Seat and it is important to make a deliberate and informed decision as to which one we choose to accept.

Boron did not coin the phrase 'Siege Perilous' (the term first appeared in the later anonymous *Perlesvaus* or *High Book of the Grail*), but whether we choose to think of the empty seat as the place originally taken by Christ or by Judas Iscariot, the message is clear: we should not idly, or through pride, assume that we have reached a further stage of spiritual development than we actually have. On the other hand, neither should we remain in such superstitious fear of the empty seat at the Round Table that we put it completely out of our minds. Boron says that the empty place will be filled by Bron's grandson, the implication being that it was reserved for future generations of Fisher Kings or Grail Guardians. When we recall that the knight who asked the right questions about the Grail and proved that he understood its meaning then became a Grail Guardian himself *through virtue of his understanding*, we might be justified in hoping that in time, we too may aspire to this.

JOURNEY TO GEMINI

Begin your journey as before. Make your contact with Gwenevere and enter the golden mist. When the mist clears, you can see the Round Table of the stars in its entirety, stretching out across the starry expanse of the night sky. You observe the constellations that you have visited, one by one. You bring to mind the long journey you have taken so far, and recognise how much you have learnt and experienced. This is truly the journey of a life-time.

Now look to your right. You can see the mysterious birthing pool of the constellation of Cancer where your journey started so long ago, rimmed with white marble and filled with swirling waters. And beyond the pool, you can see two figures standing side by side. They are holding hands, laughing and joyous, eternally youthful. They are neither male nor female, but androgynous. One of the twins appears to be human, and the other appears to be Faery. But their identity is not fixed, and you can see many latent figures within them. You can see many human and Faery partnerships.

And at times the figures take on a brightness which almost engulfs them in light. You see that one of them is Christ. And yet the other, too, is also Christ.

You ponder these Mysteries.

When you are ready, return as before.

1 Richard Hinchley Allen, *Starnames, Their Lore and Meaning* (London, Dover Publications 1963)
2 It was named by the Polish astronomer Johannes Hevelius in the 17th century AD. Its title is assumed to be a deliberate irony on the part of Hevelius who reckoned that you needed eyes like a lynx in order to see it.
3 Robert de Boron, trans. Nigel Bryant, *Merlin and the Grail* (Cambridge, D.S. Brewer, 2001) p.35
4 Ibid, p.113

CHAPTER TWELVE

The Faery Kingdom of Listenois

THE FIFTH FAERY KINGDOM is Listenois, the Grail Kingdom. Listenois lies at the centre of the five Kingdoms, and the Grail Castle lies at the centre of Listenois.

It is often thought that the stories of King Arthur and the Round Table, and the stories of the Quest for the Grail, are two quite separate things. It is said that the irresistible power of the Grail lured the bravest and best knights away from the court into a hopeless search for something so elusive that it would always remain beyond their reach, while their absence from the Round Table had a demoralising effect on those they left behind and brought about the end of the magical Order. But the fact is that the two are intimately connected. The work of the Round Table is an essential preparation to understanding the Grail, and you cannot successfully make the journey into Listenois without having first worked through the Mysteries of the Round Table and experienced the challenges of the kingdoms of Lyonesse, Sorelois, Gorre and Oriande. These, in their turn, are enriched by the spiritual energy and wisdom that flows from the realisation of the Grail and empowers the continuing work of the Order of the Round Table.

Finding the Grail is neither an insoluble detective story nor a quest of such spiritual Mystery that it can never be attained. Discovering the Grail is a matter of *understanding what it means*. When you understand what it means, you have found it. And, as was described in Chapter Two, understanding what it means starts by understanding its history. All that you need to know in order to understand the meaning of the Grail is set out in Boron's narrative, and can be learnt and experienced within the work of the court of the Round Table. You do not need to be perfect or without sin in order to realise its meaning! Finding the Grail does not rely on chance, and contrary to popular interpretation, the Grail and the Grail Castle in Listenois do not appear and disappear at random but conform to normal rules of manifestation. When you have raised your level of consciousness sufficiently, through knowledge and through the Inner understanding that comes with regular meditation and the development of spiritual awareness, and when you have explored and developed your relationship with the Faeries and their world, the castle will appear. When you return to normal waking consciousness, or if you forget or deny what you have learnt, it will disappear. The Grail can be understood by anybody who is properly prepared to comprehend its Mystery, and if you have worked through the challenges and initiations presented to you throughout this book, you have already made the preparation you need.

Of all the five Faery Kingdoms, Listenois is probably the least commonly associated with Faery, and indeed many who are familiar with the Arthurian and Grail legends might question that it (or indeed the entire mythology) has any association with Faery at all. But as we have seen from the start of this study, the Grail was intimately connected with Faery right from the beginning of its journey from the Holy Land to Avalon.

In Chapter Two, we explored the many levels of magical symbolism contained within the Round Table. First, there is the ancient, Atlantean magic brought to Britain by Merlin and which provided the foundation for the system of Inner wisdom taught and practiced within the court of the Round Table. This was based upon the concept of a quartered circle about a central point, which developed into the symbol of the perfect Rose upon an equal-armed cross. Later, as was described by Robert de Boron, the esoteric Christian ideology of the blood of Christ and the Holy Grail was added into this basic system. These two apparently disparate traditions were linked by the thread of the Mysteries specifically concerned with the relationship between Faery and human that culminated in the marriage between King Arthur and his Faery Queen Gwenevere. As Merlin explains, it is only when all three 'Round Tables' or systems of Inner wisdom are conjoined, that their full significance can be understood.

There are no further symbols, artefacts or knowledge that you need to acquire before you take the journey to Listenois: you have all you need. This kingdom represents all that you have previously experienced and learnt in the four kingdoms that surround it. Your only challenge is to dare to believe what you already know. In making this final journey, we shall follow the path taken by Gawain. If you would like to read the complete story of how Gawain reached the Grail Castle you will find it in what is known as 'The First Continuation' to Chrétien de Troyes' *Perceval: The Story of the Grail*.[1] Gawain's journey is also described in a still largely untranslated narrative entitled *Diu Crône, The Crown*.[2] The most significant episodes for the present study are described below.

THE CROSSROADS IN THE FOREST

The journey into Listenois begins in the forest that lies between the worlds. It takes place during a time in which King Arthur is absent from the court of the Round Table. The story tells how he had ridden out into his kingdom in the company of Gawain and his son, and several of the other knights of the Round Table. While he was away from the court he encountered a series of adventures that eventually led him to Castle Orgelleuse, the Castle of Pride.

On their journey back home, Gawain's son was abducted. King Arthur offered to help search for the boy but Gawain seemed strangely disinterested in looking for him. Arthur decided to send Gawain on ahead with instructions to tell Gwenevere that he would meet her at a certain crossroads in the forest within a month. In the meantime, he would continue to search for Gawain's son.

On receipt of the message, Gwenevere left the court and went into the forest, taking a large retinue of knights and servants with her. She set up camp at the crossroads, vowing that she would not move until Arthur returned. She passed the time by playing chess.

The oddities of this episode suggest that once again there is more to this than meets the eye. Gawain's son is not one of the better known knights of the Round Table, and it is strange that King Arthur decides to spend a month searching for him, especially as Gawain himself has no apparent interest in doing so. But the boy's 'abduction' reminds us of the many 'abductions' of Gwenevere that often indicate a period of time willingly spent in Faery.

Perhaps Arthur's special interest in the boy was a result of the childless state of his own marriage: he needed to find an heir. But it may also be that Gawain's apparent indifference to the fate of his son was because the child was a Faery child, and Gawain knew that the boy was safe and sound in the Faery land of his birth. His mother was a Faery, Floree, and the boy was known as 'The Fair Unknown.'

However, the result of all this is that Arthur is taken out of the action for a full moon period, and while he is searching for Gawain's son it is Gwenevere who holds the balance of power between the kingdom of Logres and the Faery realms that lie beyond its borders. In effect she is holding open the gateway between the human and Faery worlds, a vital element in the quest for the Grail as she enables the first of the knights to reach the Grail Castle.

As we have seen so often, the forest is a symbol for the lands that lie between the worlds of Faery and human, not only in the literal sense but also as a metaphor of our own consciousness. Gwenevere's game of chess is no mere pastime, but strong magic between the worlds. As we saw in Chapter Two, there is every indication that Merlin introduced this ancient magical chequer-board game into Arthur's court as an integral part of the magical symbolism of the Round Table. When Gwenevere is seated at the magical board at the crossroads in the forest, the gateway into the Grail Kingdom is opened: a magical superhighway to the heart of the Mysteries. This place where the four directions meet is the place of balance at the heart of the equal-armed cross. The four roads represent the four cardinal directions, the four elements and the four Faery Kingdoms at the quarters. Above all, it represents a place of balanced understanding within our Selves. The board, with its squares of silver and black, is a symbol of the intermingling of the Faery and human worlds, the glittering stars of the night sky and the bright crystals of the deep earth.

THE JOURNEY TO LISTENOIS

1. The Crossroads at the Heart of the Kingdom

Up until now, your journeys into Faery have started from the chamber of the Round Table, within the castle on the island at the centre of the lake. But you have reached the point in your work where you no longer need to use these Inner constructs. Your journey to Listenois begins at a crossroads that you have built in your imagination; it exists wherever you are, and it thus can be made to resonate with the land about you, wherever you happen to be. In this way you will make a direct connection between yourself, each of the four Faery kingdoms and the physical land in which you live and work. At the centre of the crossroads is your own Self. This is truly a Mystery, because it is only when you have reached this point of development in your magical work that you are able to make this a reality. To begin your journey into Listenois, you will meet Gwenevere at the crossroads in the forest, and play a game of magical chess with her.

Close your eyes in meditation, and in your mind's eye, visualise a forest all about you. Wait until you have the feel of this forest, and make it as real as you can. Then, visualise four roads leading through the forest and meeting where you stand. You know that each of the roads leads to one of the Faery Kingdoms. You can place them at their appropriate cardinal direction. These four roads meet at your own centre. Feel the place where they meet, strong and steady.

When you have built this scene in your mind's eye, you find that Gwenevere is seated under a great oak tree that stands at these crossroads. Take your time to make your contact with her. Gawain stands nearby, with several others: some are human, some are Faeries.

A green cloth has been set out on the grass in front of Gwenevere. Upon the cloth is a square chessboard, set within a wooden round. There are some tiny carved pieces on the board, some red, some white, some golden. Gwenevere invites you to join her, and you sit down opposite her on the grass, under the great oak tree.

You realise that you should not touch the pieces with your hands. As you look at the tiny carved figures more closely, you can begin to identify some of them. You see that one of the pieces represents King Arthur, and as you turn your attention to this tiny figure on the chessboard, you find that it begins to move of its own volition.

You begin to recognise other figures that you have met in your previous work at the Round Table. You realise that the board is a miniature representation of the Round Table and the Faery Kingdoms. Each of the four sides of the board corresponds to one of the four veils within the chamber of the Round Table. You can reach these kingdoms from where you are, seated at the chequered board. Simply by focusing your attention on each of them in turn, you can see them. In your mind's eye you can see the blue, watery landscape of Lyonesse. You can see a golden crown set on a green hill in Sorelois. You see the two trees, silver and gold, in the kingdom of Gorre. And you can see the Round Table, rimmed with stars, in the kingdom of Oriande.

As you gaze at each kingdom in turn, you realise that you can see, or intuit, what is happening in each of them, and you can enter any of them from where you are. You realise how closely Gwenevere is connected with them, and how much she has taught you in your exploration of their meaning. You feel familiar with them, as if you were part of them. And indeed you are, having worked through their challenges and experienced their gifts. You have earned your place at the magical chessboard that lies at the centre of the Round Table.

You find that Gwenevere recognises your achievement, and that her communication with you from now on reflects your attainment. Listen to all that she says. You are now an equal partner in the magical work between the worlds.

When you are ready to return, simply and slowly dissolve the scene in your mind's eye.

2. The Chapel in the Forest

The next important stage in the journey into Listenois takes place in a tiny stone chapel in the heart of the forest. The story describes how Gawain leaves Gwenevere at the crossroads and rides off to take up the quest for the Grail. But darkness falls, and a great storm gathers, with flashes of lightning, thunder, cold rain and such a great wind that trees are split in two. Near to death from having ridden through the storm for many hours, Gawain eventually arrives at a lonely stone chapel. The door is open, and he enters.

Inside, he finds a simple stone altar, upon which burns a candle in a golden candlestick. Behind the altar is a dark window, or mirror. Gawain hopes to shelter here for the night, but suddenly a hand emerges from the darkness and extinguishes the candle. The chapel is filled with sounds of great lamentation. Gawain rushes out into the forest, where he finds that the storm has abated and the night is clear. The sky is filled with stars.

The Chapel in the Forest takes the Seeker a significant stage nearer to the Grail Kingdom, which is already making its presence felt. By the time Gawain reached the Chapel, he had travelled a long way from the physical world and the events that take place here relate primarily to the Faery world of Listenois, not the human world that Gawain has left behind. When Gawain entered the Chapel, although those who voiced such grief were not visible to his eyes, their sorrow was so powerful that it extinguished a flame. Gawain received an unforgettable experience of something that would be a vital clue to his understanding of the Grail.

And yet it is not easy to comprehend what Gawain is being shown. The sorrow does not appear to be directly related to the death of any one particular person. The Chapel is far from the human world and there is no indication that it is dedicated to the memory of a human being. And yet the sorrow seems equally unlikely to have been caused by the 'death' of a Faery: Faeries rarely die, and even if this was the case here, we are not given any clue as to which Faery has died. All we know is that the sorrow manifests initially as a tumultuous storm that threatens to tear the forest apart, but as soon as Gawain has witnessed the sorrow, it dissipates. If we remember that the forest is a metaphor for the psyche, and is a representation of the interface between human and Faery, we can begin to understand how deeply significant this sorrow is. We are not told what Gawain learns within the Chapel, but as a direct result of his experience the storm abates and the sky clears to reveal the stars.

We must remember that these events are not literal, but metaphorical and symbolic. They are taking place within the Inner worlds and the Inner levels of consciousness. The sorrow is not of quite the same order as the normal sense of grief and loss for someone who has died, but indicates a profoundly healing shift of consciousness that takes place at a high spiritual level. The *sorrow* connected with our journey into Faery is a transformational experience, and understanding this sorrow is essential to our full understanding of the Faery race. It takes us back to the experience of the moment of the 'Fall,' when Faery and human separated, and only when Faery and human alike can touch this moment, re-living it through sorrow and then releasing it, can we freely move on.

3. The White Christ

This meditation can be undertaken either out of doors or indoors in your meditation space. Out of doors, find a special place in natural woodland or a secluded garden, perhaps where you have undertaken Faery meditations before, and where you can sit quietly without being disturbed.

Visualise the forest around you. The crossroads is now far behind you, although you know that Gwenevere is seated there, at the magical chessboard. Visualise the chapel in the forest as it has been described above. Enter the chapel. There is a low wooden bench for you to sit on. You see the altar and candle, and the dark mirror behind the altar. And now, softly repeat the words below:

Come in the name of the White Christ

You will find, in time, that One will come.

4. The Grail Castle

After leaving the chapel, Gawain continues to ride through the forest under the starry night sky, and eventually reaches the sea. A stone causeway leads out into the water. Another storm brews up, causing huge waves to crash over the causeway. Gawain is uncertain whether to continue, but his horse takes the bit between its teeth and sets off along the causeway whether Gawain likes it or not.

After some time, Gawain sees a light at the far end of the causeway. As he approaches it, it grows bigger and brighter. When he reaches it, he finds that he has entered a shining land of great and wondrous beauty. This is the Faery Kingdom of Listenois. It is like the Garden of Paradise, green, filled with sweet perfumes, and full of such joys and delights that it would fulfil the heart's desire of any man.

But Gawain soon encounters something very strange: he comes across a flaming sword of such great size that he can scarcely believe what he is seeing. The sword stands across the entrance to an enclosure. Within the enclosure is a dwelling, that has been built from crystal or clear glass. But the dwelling is empty and silent, and Gawain believes this to be an ill omen.

Gawain's passage into Listenois along the narrow causeway that takes him through deep water is familiar to us as a metaphor for the transition in consciousness that must take place before entering the Faery realms. As Gawain is nearing the powerful Grail Kingdom, his passage is more difficult, and the waters are more turbulent. It is significant that we are told that his horse took the bit between its teeth! The horse represents the instinctual 'fight or flight' reactions, the gut instincts over which we sometimes have little control. The power of the Grail, now so close, was such that Gawain was unable to stop himself rushing towards it whether he would or no.

Gawain finds himself in what seems to be Paradise. In effect, he is. We have explored the significance of this in the journey into Gorre. He then receives what is obviously a clear vision of the Garden of Eden as it is described in Genesis at the moment when Adam has been banished from the Garden for eating from the fruit of the Tree of Knowledge. A flaming sword was placed across the entrance to the Garden to prevent Adam from returning. Gawain was able to see beyond the flaming sword and into the crystalline dwelling that stood within the garden, but he realised that it was deserted. We can understand his sense of foreboding at this: it is a worryingly pessimistic comment on the future of both Faery and human races if the Garden of Paradise is no longer available to either race. But if indeed there was no hope of return to the Garden then there would be little point in Gawain continuing his journey, and we can only hope, as he did, that he would be able to achieve something that might act as a catalyst for change.

Gawain continues to ride towards the Grail Castle. He finds it surrounded by a meadow in which Faery knights are practising their skills of horsemanship purely for the delight of the accomplishment since they carry neither weapon nor shield. When they realise that Gawain has arrived, they are overjoyed that he has found his way to them.

Gawain is shown into a large hall. It is strewn with rose petals which fill it with a delicate perfume. Here is the Grail King, seated on a couch at one end of the hall. He is robed entirely in white silk embroidered with gold. At his feet sit twins, two youths, who are filled with laughter and happiness. They are seated at a magical chequer-board, and are playing a game upon it. The Grail King leans towards the board and watches their game carefully.

The hall then fills with Faery beings, and food and drink is brought to all. When all have eaten and drunk fully, a procession slowly emerges from an inner chamber. It is led by two maidens who each carry a lighted candle. They are followed by two youths who carry a spear between them. Then, two more maidens, who between them carry a salver of gold and precious stones upon a silk cloth. They are followed by another maiden, who is more beautiful than any in the world. She is richly dressed, wearing a crown of gold, and holding a reliquary of red gold and precious jewels. The procession is completed by another fair maiden, but she is weeping and full of sorrow.

The maidens place the salver on the table before the Grail King, and the youths place the spear onto the salver. The spear sheds three great drops of blood into the salver, which are taken up by the Grail King.

The crowned maiden then places the reliquary before him, which contains a wafer of bread. The Grail King breaks a third of the bread, and consumes it.[3]

Here, at the centre of the Grail Castle, we find all the symbolism that we have explored so far in our work in the court of the Round Table. Here is the perfect Rose that blooms at the heart of the five Faery Kingdoms, its petals strewn about the floor to fill the hall of the Grail King with their perfume. Here also is a direct reference to the 'twinning' or mirroring that we have found throughout our journeys. Here is the magical chequer-board introduced by Merlin into the court of the Round Table, this time played upon by the twins. This is a direct reflection and counterpart to the magical board played upon by Gwenevere at the crossroads in the forest during our journey into Listenois. The further we journey into Faery, the further we reach back into our own humanity.

Gawain, having witnessed the Grail Procession, asks the Grail King what is meant by the marvels he has seen. A great shout of joy bursts from all those gathered in the hall, who are filled with elation that someone has asked this question. But the Grail King offers him little by way of a direct reply, assuring him only that it is sufficient that h has seen the procession and sacred objects and asked what they mean. But he does tell Gawain that many of those in the Castle have now been set free from their *sorrow* as a result of his question.

He also tells Gawain a little more about those who live with him in the castle. He explains that the sorrow they had experienced was caused by an ancient conflict between two brothers, who fought over the ownership of some land. As a result of this conflict, the living were driven out of the land. The dead remained in the land, but they retained only an outward resemblance or appearance of life, while suffering great sorrow. Their only hope was in the grace of God and that one of their own kind should eventually find them and demand to know the meaning of what he had witnessed. He tells Gawain that their only desire is that this outcome should be achieved. He adds, enigmatically, that they do not yet possess all knowledge, although in many respects they are rich and lack for nothing.

The Grail King then makes a distinction between the condition which afflicts him and most of the other inhabitants of the Castle, and the maidens of the Procession. The maidens are alive, he says, but were especially chosen for their great purity to bear the penance of serving in the Grail Castle in order that once a year he could be sustained and nourished by the Grail.

This explanation given by the Grail King is perhaps the most profound description of the relationship between Faeries, humans and the land that we are likely to find, but when we look at it carefully it turns out to be rather more complex than we might initially assume. Let us take for example his statement concerning the living and the dead. When describing the result of the conflict between the two brothers, he says that as a consequence of their fight, one group of people was driven out of the land. Those that remained in the land appeared to be alive, but this was only an illusion or semblance of life rather than a reality. They experienced great sorrow, and they would only be able to move on from this condition when one of their own race found them.

But who is the Grail King referring to: human or Faery? Are we, humanity, the living while the Faeries are 'dead', having only the outward appearance of life? Or perhaps it is the Faery race that is alive, and humanity that is dead, having only the semblance of what does the Grail King mean by 'the land?' Is he referring to the whole Earth, or more specifically to the Garden of

Eden? Have we, or the Faeries, been driven from 'the land'? And who is filled with sorrow, humanity or Faery?

As we have experienced so many times in our long journey towards the Grail, we must look at this from the Faeries' point of view as well as our own. If we consider 'the land' to be the Earth, then the Grail King is explaining that humanity has driven Faery (the 'living,') from the Earth. This makes sense: we know that the Faeries have retreated into the hollow hills and to the remote islands in the astral seas. If we follow this line of reasoning through, the Grail King is saying that it is the human race that is only apparently 'alive,' filled with sorrow and only able to move on when another human being who understands the real meaning and cause of our plight is able to release us.

This seems to make sense. Our 'fall' into physicality has caused a rift in our Selves between spirit and matter which brings us great suffering. We are only able to heal that rift through the example shown to us by Christ who incarnated as Man, and through the transformational powers of the chalice of the Last Supper and the Grail which He gave to us, and from which we may be released from this separation.

And yet this cannot be quite right. We do not need to take the difficult journey into Listenois in order to be told by the mysterious Grail King what we could have learnt rather more easily at Sunday School.

We could on the other hand assume that 'the land' refers to the unfallen earth symbolised by the Garden of Eden. Gawain's vision of what is clearly a reference to the Garden just before he reaches the Grail Castle seems to confirm this interpretation. The Bible (Genesis III: 22-24) describes how Adam, the first man, was driven out from the Garden of Eden in order to prevent him from eating the fruit of the Tree of Immortality. In order to make sure that he didn't try to return, a flaming sword was set across the entrance to the Garden. In this case, although the Faeries remain in 'the land' or in other words the unfallen, Paradisal earth, they are trapped in what popular science fiction might call a time-warp: they appear to be alive but because they are separated by the flaming sword from the process of death, that occurs only outside the gate of the Garden, their appearance of life is an illusion. They lack the experience of death, change, transformation and rebirth that is only experienced by humanity, and only outside the Garden. This makes their immortality, paradoxically, a 'living death'. Without death there is no real life, but the experience of death will inevitably bring a great sorrow that will not be easy to endure.

If this is the meaning of the Grail King's words then it is only a *Faery,* 'one of their own kind,' who will be able to release them by asking the meaning of what he is being shown. The Grail King's comment that although they seem to lack for nothing they do not yet possess all knowledge is very significant at this point. He is telling us that for the most part the Faeries are not aware of their condition. They have immortality but they do not understand what that means. They will only understand, and be able to move on, when one of their own kind who comes from *outside* the special, set-apart preserve of the Grail Castle, and who has experienced life in the human world, is able to tell them about humanity and about what they do not yet understand. Such a one is Gawain, but such also are those of the human race who have increased their awareness of the Faeries to the extent that they are now able to adopt Faery consciousness. Of all the knights of the Round Table it is Gawain who, as we have seen so often, is best able to bridge the worlds between human and Faery. But as an initiate of the Mysteries of the Round Table, you now are able to take his place.

Finally, we must consider the Grail King's statement that the maidens (and presumably also the youths) in the Grail Procession were not numbered among his own kind but because of their great purity had been especially chosen as capable of taking on the burden of this great act of service. Now that we are in a position to begin to understand the nature of the responsibility they have taken on, and their task will continue until the majority of the human race has attained an awareness of Faery, we realise that they have achieved a level which transcends that of both human and Faery. We might think of them as Angels.

The conundrum posed by the Grail King is an illusion. The castle is both human and Faery, as are its inhabitants. The Grail King is both human and Faery, as is the Christ. So, also, is the one who will find them and ask the right question. If we ask the right question, it is because we already know the answer.

5. Becoming a Grail Bearer

For your final meditation, visualise the scene described above. You might find it helpful to learn and memorise the details of the procession so that you can recreate them clearly in your imagination. Use all the knowledge and abilities you have acquired so far, to make the scene come alive in your imagination.

See the Grail King, his hall filled with rose petals.

See the twins at his feet, moving the golden pieces on the magical chequer-board. Be aware that at the crossroads in the forest, Gwenevere is seated at the same magical board, the living heart of the Round Table.

Now visualise the Grail procession moving slowly before you. Visualise each individual carefully, maidens and boys, and look carefully at the sacred symbols they are carrying.

Finally, in your imagination, take your own place within the Grail procession. You carry the Grail. You offer the Grail to the Grail King. You understand what this means.

You have become a living part of this Mystery. You have the ability to take an active part in the evolution of Faery and human, to the benefit of all the earth.

1   Chrétien de Troyes, trans. Nigel Bryant, *Perceval: The Story of the Grail* (Cambridge, D. S. Brewer, 1982)

2   Heinrich von dem Türlin, *Diu Crône,* ed. G.H.F. Scholl (Stuttgart: Bibliothek de Littevarischen Vereins, Vol XXVIII, 1852).

3   Each account of the Grail Procession differs in its description of the sacred artefacts, but there is general agreement that they include a sword, spear and salver, and the mysterious Grail itself.

Bibliography

Allen, Richard Hinchley, *Starnames, Their Lore and Meaning*, London, Dover Publications, 1963

Berg, Wendy, *Red Tree, White Tree: Faeries and Humans in Partnership*, Cheltenham, Skylight Press, 2010

Robert de Boron, trans. Nigel Bryant, *Merlin and the Grail*, Cambridge, D.S. Brewer, 2001

Bryant, Nigel, *The High Book of the Grail*, Cambridge, D.S. Brewer, 1978

Chrétien de Troyes, trans Nigel Bryant, *Perceval: The Story of the Grail*, Cambridge, D.S. Brewer, 1982

Heinrich von dem Türlin, *Diu Crône*, ed. G.H.F. Scholl, Stuttgart: Bibliothek de Littevarischen Vereins, Vol XXVIII, 1852

Jobes, Gertrude and James, *Outer Space: Myths, Name Meanings, Calendars*, New York and London, The Scarecrow Press, Inc. 1964

Jones, Gwyn and Thomas, *The Mabinogion*, London: Dent, 1974

Knight, Gareth, *The Secret Tradition in Arthurian Legend*, York Beach, Weiser, 1996

Lum, Peter, *The Stars in our Heavens*, London, Thames and Hudson, 1952

Malory, Thomas, ed. Janet Cowen, *Le Morte D'Arthur*, London, Penguin Books, 1969

Wace and Lawman, trans. Judith Weiss, *The Life of King Arthur*, London, Everyman Paperback, 1997

Young, Ella, illus. Maud Gonne, *Celtic Wonder Tales*, Dublin, Maunsel and Company, 1910, reprinted London, Abela Publishing, 2010

Index

CPSIA information can be obtained at www.ICGtesting.com
Printed in the USA
BVOW05s2134220514

354166BV00001B/285/P